THE MYSTERY OF
THE CROSS

THE MYSTERY OF THE CROSS

CARDINAL BASIL HUME, OSB

Paulist Press

New York / Mahwah, NJ

First published in 1998 by
Darton, Longman and Todd Ltd
1 Spencer Court
140–142 Wandsworth High Street
London SW18 4JJ, United Kingdom

Library of Congress Control Number: 2012949218

ISBN 978-0-8091-4789-2

United States edition published in 2012 by
Paulist Press, Inc.
997 Macarthur Boulevard
Mahwah, New Jersey 07430
United States of America

www.paulistpress.com

Line drawings by Sarah John

Contents

✤

Celebrating Mystery
Christmas to Easter

Preface

✤

This book is a series of reflections on the passion of Christ and his death. They were spoken from the pulpit at different times of the year, but especially in Holy Week. Such reflections have a part to play, and an important one, in helping us to explore the inner meaning of the Mass. This is only one reason for meditating on the cross, of course. Looking prayerfully at the image of Christ dying on the cross is an essential exercise for all who are in search of God.

The book is divided into three sections. In the first, *Embracing Mystery*, the pieces reflect on the why of suffering; in the second, *Inner Peace*, the focus is on our response to suffering and the help we can gain from the spiritual life; the final section, *Celebrating Mystery*, follows the liturgical journey from Christmas to Easter. Inevitably in a book of this kind there is some repetition and I hope you will make allowance for that.

At the beginning of the book I have added a Prologue. This is a meditation prompted by reflecting on the first part of the Mass, the Liturgy of the Word. I wrote the thoughts as they occurred to me – a quick sketch, not the full picture. Similarly at the end of the book there is an Epilogue. Here are thoughts about the Liturgy of the Eucharist, again only a sketch, but maybe enough to prompt thoughts and prayer on the part of the reader.

If we meditate on the cross, on Christ's death and resurrection, then our understanding of the Eucharist will be deepened. That is, of course, a life-long task, never completed.

Basil Hume.

Prologue:
The Liturgy of the Word

The Mass is made up of two parts, the Liturgy of the Word and the Liturgy of the Eucharist. They are so closely connected with each other that together they constitute but one single act of worship. In the Mass both the table of God's Word and the table of Christ's Body are prepared, so that from them the faithful may be instructed and nourished.
(General Instruction on the Roman Missal, no. 7)

I listened to him as he spoke about God. There was a note of excitement in his voice as he dwelt upon those attributes of him who is Father, Son and Holy Spirit. He spoke of God's beauty, of his lovableness, then of his power which creates and fashions all that is. My mind strove to follow him as he tried to lead me to contemplate another reality, one that this world mirrors but not adequately so. He had known God's lovableness in a manner which eluded me, but his speaking of it warmed my heart and called my mind to go on searching, exploring – trying to soar above and beyond what I could see, hear or feel. As I write I watch a seagull going higher and higher, quickening its flight, away beyond my seeing, into another world where I cannot go. One day, he told me, you shall see him as he is, pure beauty, perfect lovableness, all powerful too.

I must bow down and adore God; praise him for the greatness that I know he embodies; thank him for all that I have and am; ask pardon from him for all that I have done to offend him and others too; ask him for the many needs that I have. We are creatures in humble adoration of the Creator, of him who made us and for whom we are made.

Then a question comes to mind. Why, I asked, must we suffer so and pain be part of our humanity? What has happened? How can we explain it?

He told me he had explored the writings of learned scholars, listened to their explanations, but had found no answer to that question which no one has yet understood. Why must we know pain, suffer and die? Can no one tell me? Is there nothing more to be said? Then one day I stopped, and abruptly so, on seeing hanging on the wall the image of a man, outstretched arms nailed to the wood, his feet too. He was dying, in agony. I had passed that crucifix a thousand times, a casual glance from time to time, but I had not seen it, not properly. That day it spoke to me, not with words of course, but its very presence was a message, a secret to be shared. There was a tale to be told, a story about a people who had been carried into slavery, who had been made to labour and to suffer, until released from their bondage. One day a Saviour would come, not to free them from

[x]

foreign invaders, nor to establish a mighty kingdom. There were greater evils than slavery in a foreign country. There was the evil of sin and separation from God. The Saviour would die for them, take upon himself the evils they had brought upon themselves. He would free them, by enduring pain and death to bring them life and an opening into a new world, where true love is experienced.

The people, now freed, must remember what God has done for them. Memories recalled and celebrated, in some manner make present now what has been done in the past for their forebears. The story has been told by the writers.

The people come now together each week to listen to that Word of God, given by the historians of old, by the holy men they call prophets, and by their poets. They come to be instructed, to recall, to learn how the past lives on in the present. Above all they come to learn more about that Saviour, God-made-man, what he said and what he did. Every Sunday the Gospel must be proclaimed, and St Paul's understanding of it read as well.

Many questions remain unanswered. How can we understand the ways of God, or discover the reason for evil and why his Son must die to save us? To fathom this mystery we would need to be like God or indeed be God himself. It cannot be. The mystery of suffering remains, a reality upon which to reflect, not one to comprehend.

Christ left us an example to follow, and words that must echo in our hearts: 'If you wish to be my disciple, you must take up your cross and follow me.' There is no hiding from that command. And St Paul told us that we must make up in our lives what is wanting in the sufferings of Christ (Colossians 1:24). Strange words indeed. The cross will be laid upon our shoulders from time to time, for some often, for others less so. The Word of God will instruct us and enable us to explore the mystery. It will prepare us to be at one with him in his sacrifice, the way to life with God and true happiness.

Embracing Mystery

❧

'The choice is between the mystery and the
   absurd.
To embrace the mystery is to discover the real.'

Recapturing a Sense of Mystery

※

In our day we need to recapture a sense of mystery. Pascal made the distinction between a mystery and a problem, and it is one we have tended to forget. A problem is an obstacle, a conundrum, something that can in principle be formulated and solved. A mystery is utterly different. It lies beyond us, it is too rich for our understanding. It can be entered into, explored, even inhabited; but it can never be exhausted or fathomed.

Our age dislikes intensely the idea of mystery, because it directly exposes our limitations. The thought that there could be something, or someone, beyond human comprehension or imagining is, of course, exciting, but it is also belittling. It puts us in our place and that place is not at the centre. Science has played an important role here, at once dispelling apparent mysteries and solving problems, and continually pushing forward the boundaries of human knowledge.

The experience of suffering and, very important, the experience of failure bring us face to face with mystery. They are stern but effective teachers of the ways of God, unless, of course, they lead to bitterness and rancour. They cause us to question our priorities, they bring a new perspective and lead us sometimes from desperation to seek and find a different meaning and purpose in our lives. Coming to us as unwelcome visitors suffering and pain can, if handled well, turn out to be friends.

❧

I am a pilgrim walking through life, and from time to time I like to think that the 'cloud of unknowing' lets a chink of light through to warm my heart and enlighten my mind. At times I find this pilgrim way not at all easy. In fact it can be pretty rough and an uphill business as I try to make my way along it. Then I hear those words: 'If you want to be my disciple, take up your cross and follow me', and I realise that I cannot get to the end of the journey except by going over that hill which they call Calvary.

So the cross is part of my life. Suffering, pain and anxiety are part of the human condition, of course, but I need to make them part of my ministry.

I had been invited to lunch one day by Pope Paul VI. While I was there one of the priests took me into the chapel and showed me a crucifix made for the Holy Father when he was Archbishop of Milan. It had no crown of thorns, and when Paul VI remarked on this to the artist he replied: 'No, the Lord has laid that on the head of the Archbishop of Milan.' When he became Paul VI the Archbishop of Milan took the crown of thorns off the head of the Lord and carried it himself.

❧

What are the Articles of Faith to you and me? They are pointers to the mystery, entries into mystery. They are starting points for endless exploration, right down the ages, and that exploration is never completed, either by the Church itself, or by us individually. One of the problems in the Church today is that there are people who think that doctrine does not evolve. But I was encouraged when I read these words by a Greek Orthodox theologian:

> We see that it is not the task of Christianity to provide easy answers to every question, but to make us progressively aware of a mystery. God is not so much the object of our knowledge as the cause of our wonder.

I have often prayed, as I am sure you have prayed: 'Lord, I do believe, help thou my unbelief.' What a marvellous prayer that is. I used to confess, from time to time, sins of doubt until I realised that doubt was my friend and not my foe. Doubt is the instrument to purify my faith. There is no growth in love unless faith is purified.

❧

Why? What is the meaning?

Sometimes, on my pilgrim way, I find myself sitting on the roadside looking round at my brothers and sisters and am appalled at the magnitude of the suffering that there is in the world. I don't think I have ever met anyone who has not been carrying deep inside them some sadness, some sorrow, and I ask myself: what is the meaning of this? I am now confessing to one of the biggest problems in my life – to know *why*. It is the biggest single proof, for me, against the existence of God. I know all the answers, but I do not understand. Many events have focused my mind on the problem. For instance, if I am sitting with a young widow who has just lost her husband, or a mother who has lost her child, the suffering seems inexplicable.

❧

A way of entering into the mystery

I have said on many occasions, in different situations, that I cannot fully explain the existence of evil and natural disasters. If I had that kind of knowledge and understanding, I would be God. But Our Lord has given us, and certainly given me, a way of entering into the mystery to try to discover some meaning, and that is his own death on the cross. It is only by looking at the crucifix that we begin to discover some kind of solution. There, and there alone, is the solution, because behind the crucifix you see, with the eyes of faith, the outline of the risen Christ. *That* is the point and that is why a crucifix is such a lovely thing.

❧

A man can have no greater love
than to lay down his life
for his friends.

John 15:13

How hard it is for us to understand why it was that
God who became man had to suffer and die in that
ignominious and cruel manner. Down the ages
Christian thinkers have reflected on these great events.
They have meditated on the words of the Gospel and
the comments of St Peter and St Paul – and yet, I
believe, the mystery is never totally explained. We
never quite see why it was that God-made-man should
have to die. Every Christian, each one of us, has to
spend a lifetime thinking about it and wondering, trying to understand just a little bit more *why* it was that
God who became man had to suffer so cruelly and die
so ignominiously.

It is just as difficult to understand the existence of
evil in a creation that was originally perfect and intend-
ed to give glory to God. We, remarkably, are the crown
of that creation made in the image and likeness of God.
Yet we have not lived up to that image. Is it perhaps
something to do with our refusal to accept God's love?

So it is that our minds, feeble and limited, simply
cannot understand all these things. But through our
faith, through that gift of his, that initiative of his, we
can begin to wonder and pray, and in our wondering
and praying find some, though only some, understanding.

But one thing is certain: the real solution to the

problem of evil – the fundamental solution to all human problems, especially sin, suffering, and death – is in his death, in his suffering, because it ended in his resurrection.

A Mother's Anguish

❦

Some years ago in Frascati in Italy, a small child, three or four years of age, fell into a mine shaft and became trapped half-way down. Rescuers worked day and night to reach the child whose helpless crying could be heard by all those who waited nearby. As the rescuers worked on, the child's mother kept vigil at the top of the shaft, anguished and distraught. The crying grew weaker as the child's life ebbed away. The world waited. The child died.

With the death of that child something nearly died in me – my trust in God's love and goodness. What had the child done to deserve such a fate? Why should that mother have to sorrow so? Every time an earthquake or some similar tragedy brings devastation to a whole village or town, whenever an innocent person is allowed to suffer, or a young person is taken away suddenly from loved ones, then for a moment I experience what I remember feeling when that small child died in the mine shaft – sorrow and helplessness.

But then the words from the psalm come back to

me: 'My God, my God, why have you forsaken me?'
These words express all the pain and anguish of a person who feels totally abandoned. Why is this happening to me? How have I deserved to be left desolate and without hope? How does one answer those questions save to recall that those words – 'My God, my God, why have you forsaken me?' – were uttered by Christ as he was dying on the cross?

If you have known utter desolation, so has Christ. And what was going through his mother's mind as she kept vigil by the cross, anguished and distraught? She shared her Son's agony as only a mother can. She watched. She waited. And Jesus died. It is hard for anyone who is not a mother to understand a mother's anguish when her child is dying.

❦

Ask the philosophers of this world why pain and suffering should be inflicted on the innocent. What have they to say for our comfort? Nothing, or little that convinces. How do theologians reconcile pain and suffering with God's love and goodness? With difficulty.

Why, Why, Why?

❦

There are moments in a nation's history when a single event unites everyone in sorrow and mourning. It happened in Britain when a terrible accident led to the deaths of many children at Aberfan in South Wales. It happened when a headmaster, Philip Lawrence, was murdered at the gate of his school in London. And it happened in Dunblane when innocent children were shot by a gunman.

What thoughts crowd into our confused minds? For my part, I think first of the anguish of mothers and fathers who have lost a child they loved so much. A celibate, such as myself, knows that he cannot enter into another's grieving for a lost child. But I would weep, and weep much, if a daughter or a son of mine had been killed at Dunblane or Aberfan or in any other way.

Words are inadequate when trying to console the bereaved. They do not, and generally cannot, mend a broken heart. Something else is needed: gestures to show love, or the sharing of a silence that can be more eloquent than a thousand fine phrases.

All the time, nonetheless, there is the question 'Why?' The problem arises in our minds that if God loves us so much, how is it that he allows something like the shooting at Dunblane to take place? It is a question I have asked myself a thousand times throughout my life. Turn to any person for an answer that satisfies, and you will be disappointed. On one of the wreaths that lay at the gate of the school at Dunblane were three words, just three: 'Why, why, why?' When asked that question 'Why?' I said we were in the presence of a great mystery, all the more baffling because we are mourning little children. By 'mystery' I mean a truth that lies beyond our understanding. So much is hidden from our eyes, so much is beyond our capacity to know and explain. I said: 'If I knew the answer I would tell you', then added: 'but if I knew the answer I would be God.' I remember the emotion I felt on the occasion of the Aberfan disaster in 1966, when a spoil heap from a coal mine engulfed the village school, and I remember saying then to myself: 'Why?' Another time I recall standing in Auschwitz and feeling the evil that still seemed to hover in that place, and again there came the question 'Why?'

❧

There are no quick answers. The mystery of God is too great, and our minds too small, too limited to understand his ways. But I cannot, and will not, doubt the love of God for every person, a love that is warm, intimate and true. I shall trust him, even when I find no human grounds for doing so. Left with the question 'Why?', I discover a light that begins to shine in the darkness, just a flicker but enough for me to say: 'I know where to look when still unable to see clearly.' I look at the figure of Christ dying on the cross. I know that if I look long enough, I shall begin to see that his passion and death have a powerful message to convey. When God became man, he accepted that he would be like one of us and would experience our darkest moments and greatest pain. What many humans have to endure, he endured. When many suffer the sense of being abandoned, he suffered that too. When many are troubled in mind, they know that he, too, was troubled in mind.

There is something important for us here. Would God, who became man, have suffered all he did were it not for our consolation and guidance, were it not to point to an answer to the question 'Why, why, why?'?

❧

I was much struck by the sermon preached by the Moderator of the General Assembly of the Church of Scotland after the air disaster over Lockerbie, when a passenger-carrying plane crashed, killing everyone on board. 'Where has God been when all this happened? Absent? Looking the other way? The Christian answer to the age-old question of why the good God permits evil, is a strange one, because the Christian faith is that God is there where we might least expect to find him, in the disaster, in the tragedy, in the suffering . . . .' Not all our questions are answered, but I found in those words food for thought, and prayer.

❧

Where did the three wise men find the one who was described as the 'infant king of the Jews'? Not in a palace in Jerusalem but in a humble and holy place in Bethlehem. They had not worked that out for themselves, but a special light, a star, had been their guide. They found him where they might least have expected to find him.

I wonder if any of those three wise men were still alive some thirty years later, and if so, what they would have made of it all if they had seen this King of the Jews – Jesus – hanging on a cross? Most certainly that is where they would least have expected to find him. What they saw, an infant, and what later they might have seen, a dying man, was not the full reality.

That infant, that dying person, was God made man for us. He became man so that a divine quality might be given to our joys and to our pains. He is in both, though we cannot see it. Our faith takes us where our reason cannot go.

❦

You ask 'Why, why, why?' and rightly so. Look at the cross, venerate it, embrace it in your prayer. Jesus had to go through darkness, pain and death so as to give meaning to our darkness, our pain and our death. But more than this: suffering and death become friends because through them we have received new life which will be ours now and after death, and for always.

God Speaks Clearly through Pain

❧

On a hospital visit I stopped by the bedside of a man who was dying. His wife was there, in tears. She was sad; she could not speak. I thought of Our Lady standing by the cross watching her Son die. Next day I had a letter from a woman saying her husband had left her. Her sadness was deep because she loved him. I thought of Our Lord, and how he felt when those who had been closest abandoned him.

Suffering comes to each one of us. We cannot escape it. The list is familiar: illness, mental anguish, old age, loneliness, heartbreak, disappointments, unkindnesses, the loss of a loved one – everyday problems no doubt, but painful experiences which can drain us of energy and take the joy out of living. It is easy to allow ourselves to become bitter and unhappy. We refuse to accept. We do not try to understand, and the pain is then worse. How do we escape from that danger?

It is, I suggest, by realising that every pain and each trial is a call from God to each one personally to become holy, to draw closer to him. God speaks clearly through pain. It is not that we should seek suffering for ourselves, that would be wrong. It is a gift from God rich in blessings and reward, but only if it makes us more Christ-like and greater lovers of our Father.

※

How can we be helped?

In times of trial we must never cease to pray. We shall be helped by Our Lord's own words and can make them our own: 'Father, if you are willing, take this cup away from me. Nevertheless, let your will be done, not mine.' (Luke 22:42). Our Lord had to struggle to say that. Or we can pray, as he did on the cross: 'My God, my God, why have you forsaken me?' (Mark 15:34). That is a powerful prayer when the trial is very great. Our Lord's suffering was so intense that he felt that even his Father no longer cared.

There will be times when we shall feel incapable of using words or, even more difficult, of having fine thoughts. It is helpful then just to sit or kneel, gazing at the crucifix. That is an excellent way of praying. You may feel wretched, overcome, sad, bewildered – but go on looking at the crucifix and it will tell you its secret. We shall understand that suffering and pain, and death as well, have now a special dignity and value precisely because Christ, who is God, experienced them.

God does not, of course, like to see us suffering and it is very difficult to understand why he allows it. It can only be because there is sin in the world. We shall only fully understand later on when we see him face to face in the Beatific Vision.

Another aspect of the secret is that Our Lord suffered and died because he wanted to prove his love for us. He had no sin, but he went as far as any person can go: he laid down his life for his friends. It is hard to show love when everything that happens to us would tempt us to become bitter and unhappy. But Our Lord did it, and so must we. We accept what God allows because we want to prove to him that we love him.

The Role of the Cross

✣

'The Son of Man is destined to suffer grievously,
  to be rejected
by the elders and chief priests and scribes
  and to be put to death.'
                                    (Luke 9:22)

The apostles found Jesus' prophecy of his suffering very difficult to understand; in fact, Peter protested. But Our Lord made it clear that he had to die, to go through his passion and death, and rise again from the dead.

We shall never understand fully why it was that Our Lord had to go through all that. But one thing is certain, that in undergoing his passion, and dying, Our Lord was identifying with us, and we know that 'the wages of sin is death'. We know that we are fallen people, sinful people, but Our Lord identified with our suffering and death, though of course in no way did he take on our sin. Because he identified with us and went through suffering and death, he made it possible for us to share in his resurrection and that life of his which we have through baptism and the other sacraments.

❦

In that Gospel passage Our Lord went on to say: 'If anyone wants to be a follower of mine, let him renounce himself and take up his cross every day and follow me.' In Lent particularly it is right that we should reflect on the role of the cross in our lives. There is no human life that is ever totally free of some suffering or pain. It may be something quite trivial, a little anxiety or worry; on the other hand, it may be something much greater and long-lasting which could be a heavy burden.

Nobody likes suffering or pain. It is wrong to look for suffering or pain for its own sake, but when it comes it plays an important role in our lives. First of all it pulls us out of the trap of thinking that this world is the only one that matters. It reminds us not to get too comfortable, not to have our sights set lower than they should be regarding what life is about or where it leads. It detaches us from our everyday concerns; that is, if we accept it in our hearts by saying, 'Not my will, but thine be done'.

It is good, too, when we have to endure suffering, to remember that we are one with Our Lord, like Simon of Cyrene helping him to carry his cross; in some way we are 'making up what is lacking in the suffering of Christ', as St Paul says (Colossians 1:24). This is a strange idea – that we in our suffering and pain can contribute to the work of Christ going on all the time.

I remember being told two things about the cross in our lives; both have been very helpful. The first is that the real cross is the one you have not chosen, the one that does not fit neatly on your shoulder. That is a very authentic cross, and very difficult to accept. The second was said by a Mother Superior to one of her community who was grumbling about the cross she had to carry: 'Don't drag your cross, carry it.' There is a lot of wisdom in that.

It is important to reflect on how we face up to the cross in our lives. In a way, we train for it during Lent by imposing some self-denial, some sacrifice, on ourselves – what we call 'giving up something for Lent'. That may sound negative and in many ways it is. But we must remember that it is done in order to help us turn to God in prayer, to focus our minds on him, and raise our hearts in desire for him. Whatever happens to us is allowed by him in order that we should draw closer to him, for that is the one thing Almighty God wants: that we should be close to him and that he should be close to us.

❦

Love's supreme example

Christ's death on the cross is proof enough of God's love for us. It takes a long time, perhaps a lifetime, to know and to understand that truth in all its depth and breadth. Perhaps only very slowly will the sight of Christ crucified on the cross give up its secret to us and enable us to understand what Christ meant when he said, 'A man can have no greater love than to lay down his life for his friends'. It is with some awe, and I trust with deep reverence, that I reread that text and speak of 'God' and not of 'man': no greater love could God have than to lay down his life for his friends. Can we say that it was almost necessary that God should become man, and as man die, to provide the greatest and most astonishing proof of his love?

The first word of the cross to us is always the word of love. And no greater love has a person than laying down his or her life for a friend. *There* is the supreme example.

The cross speaks, too, of triumph – the triumph over sin and death – because we can never look at the cross without being reminded of the resurrection. Good Friday has no meaning without Easter Sunday. Death and life were locked in conflict on Calvary. Life won because love was strong.

Life is a mixture of joy, happiness and hope, and also of sadness, sorrow and pain. Each one of us always carries that little burden which is our sins, our faults. But when we come to realise the love which Our Lord has for us, when we realise that his life revealed to us the love God has for us, then we must be filled with hope, with joy and with peace.

❦

In many ways I would like to have been at the foot of the cross as Our Lord lay dying. In many ways, but not entirely, so cruel was that death, so sad that moment. But he was offering himself to his Father, accepting his

Father's will, proving and showing in a most extreme manner the height and depth of his love – his love for his Father, his love for us.

The Crucified Christ

꘏

Pain and suffering are stern teachers of important truths which we too easily forget or ignore, namely that in this world we cannot find that complete and unending happiness for which we naturally crave. The experience of suffering, from whatever cause, can often turn us away from looking to the achievements and joys of this world for that satisfaction which we all seek.

For me one of the most moving moments in the Good Friday service is the solemn recital or proclamation of the words spoken by the dying Jesus: 'My God, my God, why hast Thou forsaken me?' What darkness of the mind did Jesus know at that moment of excruciating agony on the cross? It was, in part, the sense of apparent total futility and wastefulness of his life's work. He had failed. He was dying shamefully. And did he know then that most terrifying of experiences, the fear that after death there is nothing, just nothing? Life is indeed meaningless and absurd if its only future is nothingness. The presence of God in his life had gone from Jesus. He felt abandoned; there was no future, no hope, no God.

I have known people who have experienced that sense of abandonment. There was a young mother whose baby had died, inexplicably, in her cot. She remains inconsolable still. There was that starving child whose eyes just stared into mine, lifeless and forlorn. There was that friend made limp by doubts and tortured unreasonably by guilt. My list could go on and on, and so could yours.

To enter into a period of intense suffering, such as the mourning of a loved one, great physical pain or deep depression is like going into a dark tunnel. But if we are patient, hang on and accept it in prayer – or at least try to do so – then a glimmer of light will appear. It is the beginning of the end of that sense of being totally abandoned. It may only be a glimmer but enough to give to our pain or suffering meaning or purpose. Its meaning may be hard to see, but dimly we may perceive that to be joined with Christ in his Passion is the way to share with him in his resurrection. What does that signify? It is, from the point of view we are considering, the fact that pain and suffering cannot and will not triumph over us.

※

It is strange, and wonderful too, how God speaks to us through the ordinary events of each day. How often he teaches us to see old truths in a new and altogether fresh way. Two such events happened to me recently.

When I was visiting one of our centres in Ethiopia where people gathered in search of food, a small boy aged about ten came up to me and took hold of my hand. He rubbed it against his cheek, while with the other hand he put a finger into his mouth indicating his hunger. He made these two gestures several times. I had nothing to give and could only promise through an interpreter that I would send food to him when I got home. Eventually I had to leave the centre. As I moved away the child stood staring at me, almost reproachfully, I thought, for I had not given him food, and what love I could give I now gave no more. The look in that child's eyes has haunted me ever since. But I had learned, in a new way altogether, how there are two things we humans need above all: food and love. Without both of these we cannot live. I had understood just a little bit more clearly why the Lord chose to use bread to communicate his love for us, and to give us life.

One day I was visited by an Archbishop from the United States. We spoke about our work – its problems, its pains, and indeed about its joys too. As people so often do, we discussed the problems of our day in a manner which would be natural to two men in any walk of life. We were both aware of the woeful inadequacy we felt about our competence to cope with the many things that came our way each week. Then he said, 'Well, after all, we have nothing better to offer than what St Paul wrote to the Corinthians in the first two chapters of his first letter.' Later I went to reread them. With fresh eyes I saw what St Paul meant:

Consider the circumstances of your own calling; not many of you are wise in the world's fashion, not many powerful, not many well born. No, God has chosen what the world holds foolish so as to abash the wise ... (1 Corinthians 1:1–27)

... God's power, not man's wisdom, was to be the foundation of your faith (1 Corinthians 2:1–5)

He made holy all things that he touched. This is an ancient doctrine. He gave suffering a new importance and significance because he himself suffered. He made death a holy thing because he died. Thus suffering and death, which were the wages of sin, are now moments of grace, experiences which he sanctified and made life-giving. What a consolation it is to know that when I am lying sick, this will bring me closer to Christ. Why? He knew suffering, so sickness, being a form of suffering, has been made holy. It gives life. This would not have been so if Christ had not risen from the dead.

❧

When I sit and look at the news on the television screen, and see daily all the terrible things that are taking place in our world, it seems one of the most cogent arguments against the existence of a good and loving God. Now the evils we inflict on each other are sins and are the products of our sinful natures. These are more easily explained. But I am thinking of those other evils not of man's creation. There lies the real difficulty.

I can give no easy and quick answer to those who are bewildered or angered by some great natural disaster such as an earthquake or a tornado. As far as I know, no one has adequately and conclusively explained the existence of evil in our world. I do know, however, that the answer is to be found in looking at the crucified Christ. *There* is the book I must study to find the answer. There I shall find that Word made flesh, God who became man, suffering and dying on a cross. Like a difficult passage of text which needs time and application before its meaning is revealed to the mind, so it is with the crucifix. Slowly we see, and then only dimly, that in suffering of all kinds there is new life to be found, and therefore hope. It would not have been so if Christ had not risen from the dead.

A Vision of a Better Society

❦

M an's inhumanity to man throughout history has produced poverty, hunger, suffering and death. Conflict and wars have scarred our world for centuries. This present century, now nearing its close, has plumbed new depths of cruelty and destruction. In 1986 I stood amid the ruins of Auschwitz, the Nazi concentration camp in the heart of Poland. It was a scene of utter bleakness. Still to be seen were the remains of gas chambers and prison huts. All around me was the brooding presence of evil.

There is a part of me that recoils from speaking about my experience of visiting Auschwitz. It is a painful memory, better perhaps not mentioned. But is it just a horror confined to the past, with no meaning for us today? Auschwitz is a warning. Human beings could again destroy one another on the same scale or perhaps even a greater one.

Indeed that would seem inevitable unless we take urgent and realistic steps to root out cruelty and vio-lence wherever they are to be found. Even now in many parts of the world the destruction of human life continues. We see no end to war and bloodshed. How long will we go on destroying each other? When will we set about with single-minded energy the building of a new and different kind of civilisation?

The Holocaust ranks with the atomic bomb as evidence of what humans can do to each other in pursuit of power and damnation or in obedience to a crazed ideology.

§

Building a new world

As we come to the closing years of this millennium, people everywhere are being seized by new concerns and a new vision which in fact has its roots in an ancient faith. During the two world wars of this century the human family looked into the abyss. The 'ultimate solution' devised by the Nazis to wipe out the European Jews was the last word in wickedness. The world has now to realise that to go further along this way ends in madness and global suicide.

We have to draw back from the brink and start to build a new society where everyone recognises that we are all part each of the other. We share one home, our planet Earth. We are part of a single creation, one human family.

If ever I return to Auschwitz I would want to take with me to ponder among the ruins some words written several decades later by an American astronaut looking out from his spaceship on to our home planet.

They describe a new and positive attitude to our shared history and common future. James Urwin wrote:

> Earth reminded us of a Christmas tree ornament hanging in the blackness of space. As we got further and further away it diminished in size. Finally it shrank to the size of a marble, the most beautiful marble you can imagine. That beautiful, warm living object looked so fragile, so delicate, that if you touched it with a finger it would crumble and fall apart. Seeing this has to change a man, has to make a man appreciate the creation of God and the love of God.

If we can all begin to see our world in these terms, the insanity and cruelty of this century will never return to destroy us.

❦

Pope Paul VI used to speak about a 'civilisation of love' that had to be built in the city of man. It is a vision that gives hope. Only a dream today, but if we care enough, perhaps it will be a reality tomorrow. It could be achieved if we really wanted it and worked for it hard enough.

Thoughts of a Doctor's Son

❦

B eing a priest or a bishop is a truly wonderful vocation. It is uplifting to stand at the altar, acting *in persona Christi*, exercising his power, changing bread into his body, wine into his blood, and to be caught up in a marvellous manner into the mystery of Christ's death and resurrection. Similarly, to sit in a confessional listening to a person burdened with guilt and self-reproach and then, again *in persona Christi*, to say the words that bring relief and comfort, 'I absolve you . . .', is a rewarding experience. The priest will also anoint the sick, heal perhaps, and certainly give courage and encouragement. The priest is a shepherd, himself always restless until he has found and brought home the wayward sheep.

The doctor and the priest have much in common. Both are concerned with people, with their well-being. Our starting points may be different, but inevitably we discover that from some points of view our interests converge. The Hippocratic oath, taken by doctors, contains the words 'to cure sometimes, to heal often, to comfort always'.

⁂

The doctor now realises that a person is more than just a body, a physical reality, but is an individual whose mind and spirit make up a complex whole. The priest, for his part, recognises that a person's spirit is not something trapped within a bodily cage, that soul and body are not hostile to each other. If we see people as the sum total of interrelated cells, and no more, then our vision is partial, and therefore inadequate. If, on the other hand, we consider that the spiritual health of humans is all that matters, and that this is unrelated to bodily or psychological needs, then we treat people as angels. That, too, is a distortion and we do them harm.

The doctor's experience of people, and the priest's, tell us that many are still bewildered, indeed haunted, by the perennial problems of pain, suffering and death. Anguish in the heart, fear of dying, inner emptiness, loneliness – we have met all these, sometimes as the symptoms of sickness, quite often as the very cause of illness. They are to be found in secular society – that is, a society from which God has been banished as unnecessary or unhelpful, or one in which he is kept for Sunday and for private reflection only.

Secular society has not managed to resolve the really deep human problems. We still fear and wonder about death; we dread suffering. The consumer society – that is, the society in which we are offered every kind of material commodity and prosperity – has not satisfied the deepest longings of the human heart, or given the joy and contentment for which every heart craves. There are, too, collective 'anguishes', the great problems of the day, so clear for all to see yet so difficult to solve.

❦

Healing and renewal

Among all my patients in the second half of life, there has not been one whose problem in the last resort was not that of finding a religious outlook on life. It is safe to say that every one of them fell ill because they had lost that which the living religions of every age have given to their followers, and none of them has been really healed who did not regain his religious outlook.

(C.G. Jung, *Modern Man in Search of a Soul*)

I have often thought about that, and it has led me to reflect that what is true of the individual is surely true also of each individual in his or her relationship with others, and true therefore of society itself.

❦

Change of heart

Together we need to rediscover values that are absolute and timeless. That is no easy task. It is what the Gospel calls a 'change of heart'. It is something very radical undertaken by the individual and which must, in the end, have a profound effect on the society in which he finds himself. It consists, in part, in the discovery that what we experience in our present state on this earth is not, and cannot be, the whole story. There is a reality about which science cannot speak and which technology cannot achieve. We enter the realm of the eternal and the spiritual, the realm of religion.

❦

The 'spark' of religion ✓

It would be wrong to think of religion as concerned only with correcting evil. It has many riches to offer, indeed in the end the only riches worth having. The problems of our society, the secret fears and anguishes of the individual, all that is the dark side. We will not find solutions to these things unless we recognise and accept that religion must play a role in our personal lives, and in society as a whole. The patient may have much wrong with him but he can be healed. There are always signs of hope, always good things to note. Whatever the signs to the contrary may be, there remains in each one of us at least a spark of religion, ready to be ignited into something brighter and warmer. The promise of a healing process is there.

How do we detect this 'spark' within us? I imagine it is different in each person, which would not be a surprising fact since every person is unique. I think it has something to do with a longing deep down within us. Today we tend to speak about the search for 'meaning' and for 'fulfilment'. We want to know and to possess the good, or the good that we see in persons and objects which fall within our experience. In the end we discover that the pursuit of truth and goodness leads us to long for truth and goodness in their absolute forms. This absolute Truth and this absolute Goodness we call God. We are made for something that lies – to use our inadequate terms – above and beyond us. There is a part of every person that longs for that.

Individuals and society cannot be fundamentally healed without a radical transformation. Religion is essential to this purpose. Personal renewal and the renewal of society follow the same pattern. A return to God is a precondition for a return to health.

The Secrets of the Sea

❦

The sea, like mountains, has its secrets. One of those secrets is that the sea speaks of God. I recall a verse from the psalmist: 'They that go down to the sea in ships and occupy their business in great waters; these men see the works of the Lord and his wonders in the deep.' (Psalm 107:23–4)

There is about the sea a magnificent beauty and a terrible power. Whenever we perceive beauty or hear it around us, our minds pause to wonder whence comes that beauty, and why it pleases so much. Admiration for it gives joy and inspires song, and this is praise. If this is the effect of his creatures, and such it is, then what must he who created it be like?

The sea is never the same, the colours change, and its aspect varies, but it is always good to gaze at and moves the mind to thoughts of higher things. And what of the sea's terrible power? It has its moods, as everyone knows. In earlier times, when angry the sea taught a very salutary lesson, I suspect. It made men feel small

and dependent, fragile and in need of help. I am thinking now of St Paul who knew all the perils of ship-
wreck.

❧

If I take the wings of the morning
    and dwell in the uttermost parts of the sea,
even there thy hand shall lead me,
    and thy right hand shall hold me.
                                    (Psalm 139:9–10)

To maintain that we are being led by God all the time,
and that he is 'holding us', appears often quite contrary
to the facts as we know them and to our experience in
general. We feel for the most part, I would think, that
we move in uncharted waters with neither rudder nor
compass. Yet, if we do not believe that there is a heaven
beyond and outside this present life for which we are
ultimately destined, then life is difficult indeed and our
mood one of pessimism. Why? We have deep aspirations and limitless desires which we almost instinctive-
ly sense must be fulfilled, or else life is absurd and
certain failure.

But life is not failure. There is a gentle breeze if we
can but catch it, which blows all the time to help us on
our journey through life to our final destination. That
breeze is the Holy Spirit. But the wind cannot be
caught or used unless the sail is hoisted, and the hoist-
ing is our task. We must be on the watch, ready to

recognise it and play our part. God does hold us, and will lead us, if we want it; but we must want it.

❧

Towards the shore

Where shall we find the way along which God will lead us to discover the true meaning of all that we know and experience? Where is that fullness of life for which we pine and which we hope we shall one day enjoy? I hear the voice of the Master telling Philip: 'I am the Way, the Truth and the Life. No one can come to the Father except through me.' (John 14:6). There it is. In the person of Jesus Christ, God and man, I shall find what I am looking for. I see more clearly every day that our contemporary society has, as it were, to begin all over again. In our religious thinking we have lost too much, and we must needs rediscover the central part which Christ must play in the lives of each one of us.

We have, perhaps, tried to cross the waters relying too much on ourselves alone. Darkness has fallen, and Jesus has not yet come back to us. Meanwhile there is a strong wind blowing, and the sea is begining to grow rough. Maybe, if we look hard enough, we shall see him coming towards us, walking on the sea and drawing near to the boat. That might be a frightening experience until we hear him say: 'It is I. Do not be afraid.' (John 6:18–21).

Then we shall take him on board willingly enough; and all at once our boat will reach the land we were making for, that land where deep calls to deep. That is where God's love meets man's, and no matter what cataracts roar, or what waves and breakers roll, we shall know that we are safe, held and led to that heaven which is the vision of the Trinity – Father, Son and Holy Spirit.

Inner Peace

❦

'The wind lashes the surface of the sea
and makes it rough and turbulent,
but in the deep there is calm.'

Peace Among the Thorns

🎋

On the front page of the daily prayer book used by monks there is printed in large letters the word 'Pax', which means peace. It is to remind the monk that he is to be a man of peace. This might seem to suggest that the monk's life is one in which he escapes from the ordinary hardships and problems of everyday living. But there is more: around the word Pax is drawn a crown of thorns. It tells the monk that he must learn to wear the crown of thorns if he is to find peace within himself. This is crucial.

🎋

After Christ's death, his close followers were frightened men. After all, what had happened to their Master might also happen to them. Indeed this is precisely what occurred: each of the apostles, except John, died a violent death. Nevertheless Christ's message was 'Peace be with you; it is I. I am with you, do not be afraid.' Christ did not shirk the difficulties which came his way in life. He faced up to the fact of death. The

Christian belief in resurrection is that all the experiences which seem to be 'dying experiences' are in fact 'life-giving'. It is not by escaping from our problems that we shall find peace. No, it is by facing up to them, bravely and in a straightforward manner, that we shall discover peace deep down. The wind lashes the surface of the sea and makes it rough and turbulent, but in the deep there is calm. The wind can only strike the surface.

❧

I once visited a young woman who faced the prospect of losing her sight. She was anxious. That was natural; she would not have been human if she had not felt worried. But it did not need many minutes to discover that deep down she was at peace. That experience spoke more eloquently than any words. She wore her crown of thorns bravely, and right at the centre of herself – deep down – she had found peace. She seemed, too, to be very alive because she had something to give, something very precious. She had heard, I think, in her experiences the voice of God; she had listened and understood: 'It is I. I am with you, do not be afraid.'

Search for Meaning

❦

There is, I think, in each of us an unacknowledged struggle between the agnostic that we could so easily become and the believer that we would so much like to be. The potential believer recoils from concluding that life is meaningless and that ultimate frustration and disappointment are inevitable. The hidden agnostic is fearful lest he be deceived by arguments that do not totally convince.

That is why I like the idea of the Christian being a 'pilgrim' on the march through life, not yet at home and looking forward to a happiness which somehow seems to elude him at the present. I like, too, the idea of being in search of something. In search of what? It is not necessarily evident that the object of the search is God himself. It is in the first instance the search for meaning and the search for happiness. The human mind wants to know 'What? Why? and How?', and the mind will not be at peace until there are no more questions to be asked. It can rest only when in possession of all truth. It is the same with the human heart, that symbol of desire which is the other force that drives us to acquire and possess. It prompts our restless search for this thing or that; for the senses this is a search for pleasure, but for that higher part within us, when the good we seek is a person, we call it love.

❧

What is life about?

Our Lord said: 'And eternal life is this: to know you, the only true God, and Jesus Christ whom you have sent.' (John 17:3).

Those of you who remember the catechism will recall the question 'Why did God make you?' and the answer 'God made me to know him, love him and serve him in this world, and to be happy with him forever in the next.' That is how, for me, a very simple philosophy of life emerged, based on the need for and search for happiness. Admiring and contemplating beauty, and finding and contemplating the good which is love, seemed to point to the truth of God. It seemed to me to be the purpose of life and to correspond with what St John was saying, and with what the catechism was saying – that at the end there is God.

❧

What does that word 'God' mean to you?

There have been people, all down the ages, who have said: 'You cannot know God, you cannot have a picture of him, you cannot describe him; all the ideas we have about him are wrong, therefore all the words we use about him are wrong. You can only have a sense of nothingness, that he is there in that nothingness.'

/ So some people believe that you cannot know, or say anything valid about God. There are others who say, 'Oh yes you can, but it is always less than perfect, always inadequate.' Some people say that in the artist's work you will see something of the artist, and for me this is the nearest and best analogy. If you look at a work of art you will always see something of the artist. Some people can recognise composers: that is Mozart, for example, or that is Beethoven. We leave part of ourselves in what we create, and that is a simple thought about God: he has left part of himself in his creation. It is through *that* that we can build up our picture of what God is like. /

The Spiritual Life

❧

What is the spiritual life? It is that interior life whereby I strive to encounter God and develop my relationship with him by becoming increasingly more aware of him, and by desiring him more intensely. It involves all that I do and all that happens to me. It is the reason for my service of God and my neighbour. It is what makes me 'tick'.

For many people religion is something that concerns things outside themselves without touching their minds and hearts. So a lot of discussion on Church affairs, particularly in the media, tends to be about the institution or about the politics of the Church, or about the personalities. Someone once asked me: 'What has happened to spirituality? We don't get it from our pulpits, we don't get it in the media. With this hunger for God where do we go to be fed?' Perhaps we are too preoccupied with the earthenware vessel which is the institution, and too little concerned with the riches which the vessel contains. These riches must be discovered if we are to delight in our faith.

※

Prayer: alone with God

In recent times it has become fashionable in Christian spirituality to put great emphasis on service of our neighbour and to equate that service with prayer. There is much truth in this idea, but it is a half-truth. There can be no substitute in the spiritual life for being alone with God. There must be that part of spirituality which is private and individual – secret between me and my God. It is that daily attempt to become increasingly aware of the presence and action of God in our lives and to know the growing desire within us for some kind of closeness to him.

There must be in everybody's life an attempt to find some space in the day for prayer, however brief. It is normally in prayer that our awareness of God and our desire are awakened. It is not easy for us in contemporary Britain to find time and place to be alone with God, but the saints have taught us, and experience shows, that we all need to include space in the day and in the mind to allow God to enter into our lives. It is not always easy. We are busy people; we have many responsibilities. Our minds are preoccupied with many things. We have to make an effort to find an opportunity to be alone with God.

We can easily become discouraged if, having made

every effort to be persons of prayer, we feel that we are getting nowhere. Perhaps we expect too much to enjoy a sense of God's presence and to delight in it. When it is not thus, we feel that we have failed. It is not so. Our part is to try. God's consolations are his gift.

⁂

The garden of Gethsemane

The garden of Gethsemane is quite often – perhaps even most often – the place where we meet God; more rarely do we meet God on the mountain called Tabor where the Transfiguration of Jesus occurred. Darkness and coldness are part of the spiritual life. Every hermit knows that, and so do all who try to take prayer seriously. Love is tested by absence, and desire for God is awakened as much in periods of trial as in moments of spiritual ease. That is why so many do not persevere in prayer.

Tranquillity

❧

When visiting St Joseph's Hospice in London, I find it very moving to see how families and voluntary workers do so much to bring comfort to those who are sick. Inevitably, though, there are some people without visitors and although I try to stop at every bedside, it is especially important to spend a little more time with those who may be on their own, but who are not, I find, truly lonely. I try to offer them some words of comfort, some assurance of my own prayers and a request for their prayers in return.

I am nearly always moved by the eyes of those who suffer. So often, despite the pain, the eyes of the sick and dying can convey a remarkable inner peace. It is as if the storm disturbs only the surface of the lake while in the depths there is stillness and a certain calm. It may indeed be a hard won tranquillity.

People may have had to cope with fear and uncertainty. Yet somehow, quite often, those who suffer much are able to sense the closeness of God. They have learned to entrust the past, the present and the future to the security of a Father's love.

❦

Our story is his story, his story ours . . .

God himself, in the birth of his Son at Bethlehem, became one of us. In a new and imperfectly understood way he took our human nature to himself so that for ever more our story is his story, his story ours. This has important consequences, especially when we find it hard to credit God's love or when we might even be led to doubt his very existence.

Sometimes people wonder, when confronted by tragedy or suffering, why God lets it happen. When we are tempted to echo those words, we need to remember that God is now and forever at the heart of any human suffering. The Christ who was born under threat of death in Bethlehem and was cruelly tortured and crucified on Calvary suffers still whenever there is pain, suffering or death, among those he now identifies with. We are rightly appalled by great disasters, tragedies and famines. We can seek in vain an answer to the question 'Why?' But if we ask 'Where was God in all this?', the answer has to be, 'There, wherever there are human beings. In the midst of human pain, there, in some manner beyond our understanding, God suffers too.'

Growth in Holiness

❧

Prayer and suffering seem to be absolutely indispensable if we are to try to grow in the love of God. Our Lord himself said that to be a follower of his you had to take up your cross and follow him. From time to time in our lives we all have to play the role of Simon of Cyrene. That is one of the reasons St Paul gives in that very curious phrase, 'to make up what is wanting in the suffering of Christ' (Colossians 1:24). I have never known exactly what that meant, but it is obviously not only extremely important but also a fact.

❧

The small hurts of daily life

I don't know about you, but in my experience there are quite a number of daily hurts that are part of life, and as far as I am personally concerned, I think about a dozen missed opportunities occur every day. It is important to see the small hurts that happen each day as a call from God to turn to him. Sometimes he cannot get through without shouting very loud and clear, and the most effective way of shouting is to pull us up short. Suffering is one of those ways. All those small things that can come our way – feeling neglected, feeling there are those who despise us, the sense of being criticised unfairly – those are the sort of things that leave a hurt, not a big hurt, but a little one.

How do we use such moments? It is astonishing how a little hurt can cause quite an explosion inside of anger and fury with the other person because they have despised or criticised us. I am sure there is only one way to turn something destructive into something positive and that is to realise it is a real self-emptying when those things happen. It is good then just to go down on your knees in prayer. I remember some time ago, when someone said something that was a real snub and made me feel extremely wild inside and very humiliated. But, uncharacteristically, I went into church and thanked God for it, and to my astonishment came out feeling good.

※

Spiritual trials and prayer

When people are in great physical pain or mental anguish they are unable to pray, until they find out that in it all Our Lord is with them. I am sure that the only prayer a dying person is capable of is to kiss the wounds of Our Lord.

The spiritual authors all suggest that if you are experiencing dryness in prayer, and going through difficulties spiritually, then it is important to check your own life to see if there is any conscious barrier between you and the Lord which is displeasing to him. As well as that, there are the everyday spiritual trials, the darkness we often go through, and the doubts. Whatever the cause of our difficulty, just as when humiliations come, we should kneel down and say thank you to God. When pain and anguish overwhelm us, we kiss the wounds of Our Lord; so too, when spiritual trials occur, then in the darkness we say: 'Lord, I do believe; help thou my unbelief.'

Hunger for Love

A mong my memories of being among starving people in Ethiopia, two things in particular have struck me. The first is this: when people have nothing, when they have lost everything, their basic needs become very clear and simple. Such people hunger for food and for love. They crave to have their bodily needs satisfied, but they crave, too, to be wanted and valued. The other deep impression was of men and women of very different faiths and backgrounds striving hard to meet these two needs in those starving people.

I remember a particular nun, aged about eighty-five, who had spent many years in China, and had been in prison for her beliefs. She invited me to 'come and see my special friends'. They were living in a shack, and those special friends were not only starving but were also handicapped. Some people might say: 'Are they the ones to be saved? Should they be among the priorities?' But for that nun they were very special. She had no food to give them, but poured out love on each one.

Unable to feed their bodies, she was feeding their spirits. I did not think I would have to travel so far to see someone living the Gospel in so pure a fashion.

Watching her, I found it easier, and more honest, to identify not with her but with those starving people, the handicapped and the blind. I mean that they expressed that hunger for meaning and for purpose in life, the hunger for ultimate explanations, the hunger for absolute love, which we recognise as the hunger for love.

I saw in those people the hunger that is in every human heart: to love completely and be completely loved. To love permanently and totally. It was in Ethiopia that I realised that words like 'permanently' and 'totally' do not belong to this world, but to the next. There are hints of it in our human experience, but the reality is for another time.

❧

Poverty in our material lives

I looked into the eyes of a very old man. He was dying. He had no food, no home. He had nothing, yet he had everything because he was filled with God and so was at peace. He was serene. He was rich. I have often thought about him, among the starving in Ethiopia, and wondered how it would be if our roles were reversed. How would he see us in the Western world? Would he not find us starving too? Which of us was to be pitied most, him or me? Perhaps the answer is in the words he might say to us in the Western world:

> You do not give yourselves time. You are so busy, you have no space just to be, because you are so preoccupied in doing things. You are rich in material things, but are you rich in spiritual things? Have you discovered what true love is? Have you any idea where it is to be found?

I have an idea he would say to me, 'You are the blind one, the handicapped one', and I like to think I would then hear a voice saying to me, 'What would you have me do for you?' Remember the marvellous scene when Our Lord asked this of the blind man at the side of the road, who answered, 'Lord, that I may see' (Mark 10:51). That scene became most real for me as I lived through that extraordinary Ethiopian experience.

To see what? I would want to see Jesus Christ – my way, my truth, my life. I would say to Our Lord: 'Yes, I have read a lot, discussed a lot, argued with my friends, and I still want to know what God is really like. I must know because I must find true meaning and purpose in life.' I think the answer would be:

> 'He who sees me, sees the Father.'

Our Woundedness

I go through life as a pilgrim, a pilgrim who limps, which means that I go through life as a wounded pilgrim. It is very important to know one's woundedness and to accept it. I don't think I have ever met a person who was not in some way wounded, whether by their background, their upbringing, early disappointments, something that has happened to them or something they have done.

If you were lying on a psychiatrist's couch, his purpose would be to let you come to terms with your woundedness. A spiritual guide would go along with that of course, but would also want to reassure you that your woundedness is part of you. Just as our hearts go out to the handicapped, to those we see around us who are in need and who are wounded, so I believe it is true that there is a soft spot in the heart of God for the wounded and handicapped.

Our woundedness is a reminder all the time that the Lord walks with us, touching and healing if he wishes, but helping us to bear it if he decides not to heal us.

People who think they are not wounded are people

who are arrogant, self-satisfied, people who think they do not need God. That is rather terrifying. Look at your own life and you will find that somewhere there is a wound. I say that because as I go searching and journeying through life, looking for meaning and purpose, and ultimately looking for God, I know that often I do not see or hear; I know that there is a kind of paralysis within me. I don't know how to move forward and don't know where to go. That is why I find so much in the Gospels to be immediately helpful and immensely consoling.

❦

Needs and aspirations

When I journey to discover my needs, then I think I have understood something about God. When I journey to discover what my aspirations are, then, too, I think I have discovered something about God. I think I feel deeply the need to be healed: as long as I have those wounds, I remain unfinished, incomplete. I know that I need forgiveness: none of us has been the kind of person we would want to be. I know that I need understanding. I know that at times I need to be consoled, because life can be rough and difficult.

I have discovered in my life that I have never really met anybody who could understand me as I wish to be understood, who would give me that kind of forgiveness which, deep down, I feel I want, who could give me that total healing, and console me in my need. The person who will understand, who will heal, forgive and console – *that* is my view of God.

How do I know that? Because I go to the Gospel and see how Our Lord understood people, how he forgave them, healed them and consoled them. Our Lord is God, and as we read in St John: 'He who sees me, sees the Father.' (14:9). He reveals in that human way realities and truths about God which we could not know, or guess at, in any other way. Reading the Gospel and seeing how Our Lord understood, healed, forgave and consoled, I find that God's attitude is revealed, and it makes me warm towards him.

Our Blessed Lady

꽃

Strong in faith, generous in love, cheerful in hope

Our Lady played a key role in the life of Our Lord which earned her the great title of Mother of God. She plays an important role now in the life of the Church and is increasingly called Mother of the Church, the Church that was born on Calvary and received its mission at Pentecost. She was there on Calvary suffering birth pangs, as it were, as the Church was born from the pierced side of Our Blessed Lord. She was present in the Upper Room when the Holy Spirit came down on the apostles.

She is Mother, always there, always interested, always available – a bit in the background, but constantly there. We are reminded of her presence whenever a feast of hers takes place.

Has it occurred to you to consider that Mary (though it seems odd to put it this way), the most distinguished of all the followers of Christ, was a lay person? Has it occurred to you that she whose heart was pierced by a sword, she who suffered most closely with her Son, was not in fact a martyr? But of all those who followed after, none was stronger in faith, more generous in charity and, I would suggest, more cheerful in hope.

※

Our Lord went out of his way to praise her faith and her love. How could there be a greater vocation than to bring the Son of God, himself truly God, into the world to be at the same time truly man, and to care for him and help him prepare for his work? But the true value of a person lies in the way that person listens to God and is prepared to respond by wanting the things God wants. And what is this listening and this mutual wanting but the basis of true love? The future was hidden from Mary. There was much she did not understand. She would suffer, see her husband die and her only child leave home. She had to cope with the ordinary worries and anxieties of everyday living and then the real trial: those last days and hours when she stood at the foot of the cross. But she believed and she loved, so she trusted.

※

Our help in times of sorrow

Whenever I see on the news the anguished face of a mother as she cradles her dead child in her arms, I find it almost impossible to imagine what that mother may be experiencing. She suffers for her child; she suffers with her child.

I remember once trying to comfort the mother of a beautiful teenage girl who had been killed in a road accident. I could only sit with her in silence because no words of mine seemed to be of any help. We never cease to be children of our mothers however old we are. When we suffer, they suffer too.

So it was with Mary the Mother of Jesus: she stood at the foot of the cross and shared the agony of her Son. As he was dying, he gave his mother to be St John's mother. It was just a simple gesture. At that moment we were all being represented by St John, he was each one of us, so to speak. This explains the unique role played by Mary in the lives of Christians, the family of those reconciled to God through the passion and death of Christ: Mary his Mother is our Mother also. Art and other forms of devotion down the ages have tried to express this truth of Mary as Mother. A notable example is the sculpture in St Peter's in Rome, fashioned by Michelangelo, which represents Mary cradling her dead Son in her arms.

When mothers grieve, they have in Mary one who understands and wants to comfort; a mother like them, a mother for them. I think it helped when I tried to explain – rather haltingly, I admit – to that mother mourning the loss of her child, that Mary was there to comfort her. I think Mary did.

The Dark, Silent Tunnel

❧

One Ash Wednesday I was motoring up the A1 on
my way to give a lecture. Intending to listen to
the news, I turned on the radio and heard with
joy the familiar strains of Allegri's Miserere. It was quite
beautiful. Unfortunately, reception was marred by my
having to pass under a series of bridges and you know
how that acts like a dam in the flow of the music.

Such music and song, superbly performed, raises the
spirit and lifts the thoughts into a world of pure beauty where it is good to rest and just be there.
Experiences like this are happy reminders that the
journey through life, often dull and monotonous like
driving on a motorway, is tolerable if the end of the
journey will bring happiness and fulfilment. They are
pleasant reminders, too, that Ash Wednesday is not the
norm. Easter Sunday is.

❧

The end of the journey: I believe it is good to think
often about how it will be when our journey through

life has been completed. Of course, we must keep our eyes on the present road, trying to improve it and make it as easy for others as we would like it to be for ourselves. But what happens at the end? Quite simply, we shall see God as he is in himself. That will be a moment of ecstasy, the perfect union of our limitless capacity to love with that which is most lovable. The sight of that which is most beautiful will call forth from us a song of endless joy, a song born of wonder and admiration. We shall have achieved that perfection for which we were made: to love God, and all persons in him, and to praise him in his glory for all time.

To say that we are destined to see God one day, and that this vision of God will be our eternal happiness, may seem a little unreal to us at present. Indeed the whole business of praising him here and now may well appear to be a less than worthwhile occupation. What do we know of the glory of God when we have never seen him with our own eyes or heard his voice with our ears? We need ears to hear with, and eyes that can see, and then we shall see much; we shall not, however, see God as he is in himself but the divine translated, so to speak, into human terms. 'Show us the Father' Philip said at the Last Supper. 'He who sees me, sees the Father' Our Lord replied (John 14:8–9). So we have already seen much, but not yet everything. We must still wait to see the beauty of God, which is the prototype and source of all that we call beautiful.

❦

Shafts from the glory of God

Look through a microscope and see the marvellous composition and pattern in the smallest cell. Search the skies with a telescope and study the stars and constellations that you will find there. Reflect upon your best and noblest experiences. Observe the experiences of others; read about them in literature. In all this you will glimpse what it means to be made in the image and likeness of God.

Listen to the pure note of a violin, or the skilled rendering of a choir's song. These too provide glimpses of that beauty which is God. Each speaks with an eloquence which is its own, but all of them are also eloquent expressions of him who speaks through them.

Man is made to love God and to praise him. These two are closely related. When we accomplish them, then we are truly ourselves. That will most certainly come about at the end of our journey – unless, alas, we deliberately decide now to turn away from God. But here on earth such praise of God will not come naturally and inevitably. There are forces and factors within us that will lead us along false ways. On our journey through life we constantly have to train and prepare for our everlasting life's work.

There are sure to be times in life when, with our sight dimmed and our hearing impaired, praising God will seem artificial and unrewarding. These are precisely the moments for renewing our efforts and pursuing our journey, not for giving up the struggle. These are bridges over our personal motorways which temporarily cut off God's music as it comes to us through the atmosphere. But we must drive on through the dark, silent tunnel until, on emerging, God's music is heard once more, clear and beautiful.

Facing the Unknown

❧

It was not easy to leave my monastery; it is never easy to leave home. The most difficult part was leaving all the people I had known for so long and had grown to love and respect. More than three hundred years ago a Frenchman wrote: 'Going away is a kind of dying.' So it is. There is pain and fear of the unknown, and a certain darkness threatening the spirit.

I know my experience is an everyday human experience. How much worse it is for those who have to leave their jobs, or who lose them, with all the uncertainty that can bring. I think of the man who has to leave his home and friends, and take his wife and family into the unknown. What a worry that can be; what darkness he may know, what uncertainty. This, and so much more, is the lot of millions of people today.

❧

Every religion must offer some account of this dark side of life. For the Christian the darkness is penetrated and overcome by Jesus. Compelled by his love of God and of mankind, Jesus entered into our darkness. It is my conviction, borne out in my experience and in the experience of many others, that I meet him in the dark places on my journey through life. Perhaps it would be truer to say that he finds me there.

Christ's death was not a final darkness. It was a beginning. It led to life. He is risen: that is the full Easter message. When I meet him in my darkness, it is the risen Jesus that I meet, bearing his gift of resurrection to me with all the joy and peace that this means. I am confident that death leads to life, whether it is the little deaths we die each day, or that last change which is death itself.

Whatever our problems or uncertainties, however dark the future may seem, we can always go forward bravely into the unknown. Jesus Christ experienced this darkness himself, but through it he encountered light; he rose from the dead. That is the main reason why we should be joyful and at peace.

Beyond Death

T here is no greater evidence of our being subject to limitation than death. It asks questions of a very fundamental kind. Why should it happen? Is it the end of everything? Can we hold it off indefinitely?

One of my earliest childhood memories was the sight of a coffin being borne through the streets of Newcastle to its final resting place. Dimly I can still see the scene in my mind's eye. My thoughts at the time were doubtless childish ones – uninformed, naive even. But the incident was a starting point, an experience which over the years led to more reflection and speculation.

It provoked within me then the realisation of how short life is, even for those who live to a great age. I found myself unable to believe that it all ends in a grave six foot under the ground or in the clinical surroundings of a crematorium. In everyone there is always a strong urge to go on, a refusal to accept a return to the nothingness whence we originally came.

I further reflected that if life is short, or at least relatively so, then surely it is foolish to trivialise it, make a nonsense of it or believe it to be inherently absurd. Such thoughts were the begining of a lifelong search for the meaning and purpose not only of my own life but of every human life of which death seems to make such a mockery. It never seemed right to me that death should be the end, the final irrevocable act. Human life for me has always pointed beyond; it makes sense only if it is a prelude to and foretaste of a richer, more lasting existence.

Physical death, part of the endless cycle of decay and regeneration in the natural order, has its own beauty and inevitability. I came gradually to accept that our human denial of death, our constant flight from it and our fear of it, are evidence that the human spirit, our deepest identity and individuality, belongs to a different order of reality. We are in part imperishable.

※

Death, the gateway to a better place*

We ask why, why? We did so at Dunblane and at Aberfan. We do so now on the death of Diana, Princess of Wales.

Death is a formidable foe until we learn to make it a friend. Death is to be feared if we do not learn to welcome it. Death is the ultimate absurdity if we do not see it as fulfilment. Death haunts us when viewed as a

* This reflection was given following the death of Diana, Princess of Wales.

journey into nothingness rather than a pilgrimage to a place where true happiness is to be found.

The human mind cannot understand death. We face it with fear and uncertainty, revulsion even; or we turn away from the thought for it is too hard to bear. But faith gives answers when reason fails. The strong instinct to live points to immortality. Faith admits us into death's secrets. Death is not the end of the road, but a gateway to a better place. It is in this place that our noblest aspirations will be realised. It is here that we will understand how our experiences of goodness, love, beauty and joy are realities which exist perfectly in God. It is in heaven that we shall rest in him and our hearts will be restless until they rest in God.

We, left to continue our pilgrimage through life, weep and mourn. Sadness reigns in our hearts. You, Diana, and your companions too, are on your way to union with him who loves you so. He knows the love which you, Diana, had for others. God speaks now of his love for you. Our tears will not be bitter ones now but a gentle weeping to rob our sadness of its agony and lead at last to peace, peace with God.

Celebrating Mystery

Christmas to Easter

The Mystery of the Incarnation

❧

Christmas: what are we celebrating?

The birth of Jesus means that Jesus Christ became man. That is the most astonishing truth. It is the central truth of the Christian faith. The birth of Jesus Christ means for us that the power of God, his love and life, his very self, became flesh and blood. From that moment onwards God has thrown in his lot with us. Now one of us, he shares our living and loving, our joys and miseries, even the agonies of death. It is in Christ that the human and the divine meet.

❧

Children – instinctively spiritual

Setting a child before his disciples, Our Lord said: 'Unless you become again as little children you will not enter the Kingdom of heaven.' (Matthew 18:3). Picture a child kneeling at the crib, and watch the face of that child. It has an expression of wonder and delight. The child has listened to the story again and again, and here, in visual form at the crib, it is told once more.

A child kneels naturally before the crib, and we too must learn to surrender our independence – the control we think we have over our lives. Unless we can kneel before the wonders of God like a child, and be open to the guidance of the Holy Spirit, we remain like children, unfulfilled. Believing is not credulity; it is not childish. Believing is accepting as true what we have been told by one whose knowledge and integrity we trust. It is what Jesus himself has told us about himself, preserved for us in and by the Church.

A Christmas Meditation: 'The Visitor'

🌿

H e noticed, for the first time, the tower of the cathedral climbing high into the darkness. It suddenly began to draw him like a magnet. He felt compelled to enter, just to look. Even now he does not know why this should have been. He didn't usually enter any church. If the truth be told, churches and all they stood for had no relevance as far as he was concerned. Indeed, he thought, what good had religion ever done, save to set man against man?

His eye was drawn at once to the cross that hangs from the dome and seems to fill, even obtrusively so, the great empty space that is above. He was taken aback at the sight of it – a man on a gibbet, tortured, abandoned, dead. He had seen terrible sights, or at least pictures of them – men, women, even children, slaughtered in Bosnia and other places of conflict. They, too, were abandoned. He wondered who this man might be, dead on a cross. Why had he deserved so terrible a fate?

Our visitor lowered his eyes to the altar beneath, in contrast ornate, not without beauty. It was like a table, prepared for an honoured and much esteemed guest, no doubt to celebrate some great occasion. Later he learned that the altar, so like a table, and the cross above it, were indeed linked, not to remind of death but to celebrate life and hope.

The visitor made his way up the north aisle, past several chapels, until he reached one where the crib was to be found. Kneeling at the crib was a child, a girl of seven or perhaps less. He thought to ask her why she knelt, but instead said: 'Who is that baby?'

'That is Jesus,' she answered.

'Why is he lying there in a stable?'

' 'Cos the inn was full, and his mum was poor.'

'What happened to the baby later on?'

The little girl looked at him, half in pity, half in amazement, for he had asked, so she thought at any rate, a foolish question. He should have known. 'Why, he died on a cross,' she said.

'Where is he now?' the visitor asked.

'In heaven, of course. He didn't stay dead.' She might have added 'silly' but she didn't. Good manners triumphed.

He looked at the child, and the child looked at him, adding, he thought rather patronisingly, 'And we won't stay dead either.'

The visitor, for his part, felt increasingly irritated by the child's certainty; or was it credulity, he asked himself. He wanted to react, petulantly, but checked himself. Good manners prevailed once more. He brooded. Had he felt annoyed because the child knew something that he did not? She seemed so certain. Didn't he want certainty about the meaning of life, and didn't he want to know where death fitted in? He had a sneaking feeling that the child possessed some knowledge hidden to himself – and not only the child. There were men and women at prayer all around him. Unlike those who wandered around, they were still, at peace, it seemed. They appeared to be in possession of a secret, a precious secret. He envied them.

He went on sitting, thinking, brooding. Then he heard singing. It came from far away, from behind that cross and that altar. It was quite beautiful. As he listened, his mind and heart seemed to be carried upwards into another sphere of reality. For the first time in his life he was at prayer: nothing complicated, nothing dramatic – just the sense of reaching out in thought and desire. He was not sure how to describe it. He knew he was being drawn to look beyond the horizons of today's problems and tasks to something else – or was it not somebody else? He stayed, thinking, brooding, realising his emptiness, acknowledging his poverty, confessing his desire to be enriched – indeed, to be saved.

Yes, he was searching in prayer for something, or someone, to give meaning and purpose to his life. They call it faith, the conviction that there is a reality that is above and beyond our limited human minds, truths that we could not discover for ourselves. Did that child in the crib come to tell us all about that? And had not that other child, looking at the crib with eyes of wonder and joy, taught our visitor an important lesson?

The Tabor Experience

🌺

The Tabor experience was both fulfilment and foretaste. On the mountain which was ablaze with God's glory, Moses and Elijah spoke with the transfigured Christ. They stood alongside the Son of Man soon to be revealed as the Man of Sorrows. Moses was in search of God, and at prayer on Mount Horeb he had begged to see the glory of God. He was told that no one could see God and live. He was not to see God but only to catch a glimpse of the glory as God passed by.

Moses' experience is one that we share. We may long to see God and cannot do so directly. Nonetheless we search for him and at times we, too, catch a glimpse of the glory reflected in what is true, good and beautiful. For believers, of course, there is the assurance that we see the revelation of God in Jesus Christ, for to see him is indeed to see the Father.

On the same mountain of Horeb, Elijah was to encounter God.* He had endured bad times and was in

* For the stories of Moses and Elijah on Mount Horeb, see Exodus 33:18–23 and 1 Kings 19.

[82]

a very depressed state of mind. God was revealed to him not in the mighty storm that split mountains and shattered rocks, nor in the earthquake or the raging fire, but instead in the gentle sound of stillness. In our lives too, we can often best experience God not in extra-ordinary and shattering events but when we are silent and still. At such times we can be most completely our-selves and open to the Holy Spirit who is at work imperceptably within us, shedding light on our minds and warming our hearts.

Peter, James and John fell to their knees on Tabor, marvelling at the sight of Moses and their transfigured Lord. They saw the glory of the divine shining forth in the human. Then as the brightness faded, they saw only Jesus. Once again the human face of Christ was veiled, concealing from sight the radiance of his inner divine glory. As they descended the mountain, a new chapter was to begin. Our Lord set about teaching them: ' "The Son of Man will be delivered into the hands of men; they will put him to death; and three days after he has been put to death he will rise again." But they did not understand what he said and were afraid to ask him.' (Mark 9:31–2).

❧

Suffering leads to new life

Few of us are brave enough to confront pain or impending disaster. We run from reality or take refuge in distractions. We do not make the connection between suffering and new life. The disciples, like us, did not understand why the towering figure of the Son of Man, as foretold in the Book of Daniel, should be killed, and still less how he could rise again. Even after the resurrection, many found it difficult to grasp the meaning and purpose of the death of Christ.

Tabor and Calvary are linked in the Gospel and are linked also in life. We long for the experience of transfiguration, to stand on Mount Tabor with Peter, James and John and to see God revealed in Jesus Christ. We want to be like Moses and catch a glimpse of his glory. We want, like Elijah, to hear God in the sound of stillness. But the magnificence of the Son of God transfigured on Tabor is to be found veiled in Gethsemane and on Calvary. The glory of God, not now seen directly by human eyes, is just as real and present when Christ experiences agony in the garden. In this agony of the Son of Man all humankind was involved. The passion of Jesus Christ is for all time and all people.

St Matthew records Our Lord's teaching that he is to be seen in the hungry, the thirsty, the stranger, the naked, the outcast. Christ, then, still suffers today. Of human suffering there seems no end. The passion and death of Christ is everywhere echoed and continued. St Paul tells us that in our pain and anguish we make up for what is wanting in the suffering of Christ. These are profound and mysterious words whose meaning we still ponder.

Tabor and Calvary, in their different ways, reveal the true face of Christ who is the Son of Man and the Man of Sorrows. But there was to be, as we all know, a further revelation when the crucified became the risen Lord. It was then that suffering humanity was shown its ultimate destiny and meaning. Death and suffering were swallowed up in glory.

Life everlasting and love without end became the themes of the Good News which is the only hope for humankind. We who still live in the valley of death and darkness should lift up our eyes to where the day has already dawned, and where Christ, the Son of Man, is seated at the right hand of the Father in eternal glory.

The Temptations of Our Lord

❦

At times during our lives, like Our Lord, we too
need to live for forty days in the desert, to
attend more closely to God and to purify our
hearts. Each year we penetrate more deeply, and share
more fully, the mystery of divine life and love revealed
in the death, resurrection and ascension of Our Lord
Jesus Christ. During Lent we reflect on the mystery by
recalling the three temptations of Our Lord after his
forty days of fasting and prayer.

The temptations of Christ reveal the human condition. They tell us something about faith and hope
and the sovereignty of God over the whole of
creation. First, the devil took advantage of Jesus'
hunger after forty days of fasting to tempt him to
limit his concern to the relief of physical human need:
giving bread to the hungry, drink to the thirsty, cloth-
ing the naked, housing the homeless. These are vital
concerns and God cares about them, but they cannot
be the sole concern of the Saviour or of the Church
which continues his mission. We need too a reason for
living, a sense of purpose, a vision. We need the bread

of life, the word of truth which comes from God. The best gift to the world is the revelation of God in Jesus Christ.

The second temptation was to seek a sign from the Father, a dramatic intervention to overwhelm all disbelief and opposition. On Calvary there was an echo of the same temptation: 'Let him come down from the cross now, and we will believe in him.' (Matthew 27:42). But miraculous escape is a delusion. The children of God have to be prepared to wait in faith and enduring hope. We realise, like Christ, that love alone will conquer hate and that life is found only in the experience of death. In darkness we have faith in the light, we hope for life without end. Despair paralyses the human will. Instead, we are offered the inspiration of hope and new life.

The final temptation is to use earthly power and strength to enforce the good we wish to achieve. But, whatever the motive, we must follow the path God the Father has shown us in the life of his Son. In faith and hope we must be content with weakness and apparent failure. The blessing we bring to our world is the message of Jesus Christ, a message that we must communicate and put into practice. It is the only answer to the unbelief and moral anarchy that causes so much misery.

It is our task to witness to the truth and commit ourselves to the Gospel of reconciliation, peace, unity and love of others. We must be consistent and wholehearted in our service of God.

Holy Week

❧

In Holy Week we think about the passion, death and resurrection of Our Lord. We are not merely recalling historical events. We are not just re-enacting a pageant with no meaning. We are remembering and reflecting on these events in order that we may ourselves participate in the work of Christ. Our Lord was offering himself to God his Father, offering his love which he expressed through obedience – an obedience which included the acceptance of death. At the same time, he was passing through death to life so that you and I might share in his risen life.

We have to be involved in the offering of love which Christ made on the cross. In the sacrifice of the Mass we are provided with that opportunity. Through the sacraments, especially the Eucharist, we receive the risen life of Christ; indeed, in Holy Communion we receive the very author of that life.

❧

Our chief thought on Maundy Thursday is the institution of the Mass. On Good Friday we think of the offering Our Lord made of himself to his heavenly Father.
On Holy Saturday we think of that risen life in which
we share. In a sense, every time the Mass is celebrated,
Holy Week is contained in its entirety.

Maundy Thursday

❦

Evening Mass of the Lord's Supper

I was once invited by some Jewish friends to celebrate a Passover meal with them. In Jewish homes
this is always a festive occasion, a happy time when
families and neighbours come together. There is prayer,
the reading of Scriptures, song and laughter too.

Why is the Passover celebrated? As one Jewish
author has written: 'It is a night when every Jew should
regard himself as though *he* were freed from Egyptian
slavery and began the march from the land of his
bondage towards Sinai where Israel would receive the
gift of the Ten Commandments.'

My evening was a very pleasant one, but also very
moving. I kept thinking about Our Lord, how he had
sent Peter and John to prepare the paschal meal and
then sat down to celebrate with his twelve disciples.
His opening words, according to St Luke, were: 'I have
longed and longed to share this paschal meal with you
before my Passion. I tell you, I shall not eat it again until
it finds its fulfilment in the Kingdom of God.' (Luke
22:15–16).

At that Passover meal I ate the same food as Our Lord ate at the Last Supper: unleavened bread, bitter herbs to remind us of the days of slavery in Egypt, and an egg to signify the emergence of life from death. As was customary, we drank four cups of wine. We sang the same psalms as Our Lord sang, called the *Hallel*, at the end of the meal. I listened to the little children asking their father why this night was special, and to the beautiful answer given: 'It is still our duty to tell again the wonderful story of our departure from Egypt, about the escape, about the Red Sea, about the wandering in the desert.' We were all reminded that we celebrated those important events as if we had been personally present.

I wondered at what point Our Lord had taken bread and, as we did on that night, blessed and broke it. But here was the difference, for he said: 'This is my body which will be given for you.' No longer bread, but his body, to be rendered lifeless on the next day, the day we call Good Friday. Then he took the cup of wine and said: 'This cup is the new covenant in my blood which will be poured out for you.' (Luke 22:19–20).

I could not help but wonder, too, at what point he leant over and handed a morsel of unleavened bread with bitter herbs to Judas. Poor Judas, he had treachery in his heart, not love.

❧

Our Lord's action with the bread and wine changed everything. The great event for us now is not the flight from Egypt, though we remember that too with gratitude along with our Jewish brothers and sisters. Their deep religious sense enabled them to see in these events great truths about God – their God, our God – his claims on us and our response to him. But the event we now celebrate, and do so at every Mass, is that other exodus, the passion, death and resurrection of Our Lord. Why? Because he told us to 'do this in commemoration of me'. At every Mass we are involved totally, even if at times unknowingly, in what Christ did for us through his death and resurrection, the great liberation from sin and death. Always at Mass there is thanksgiving in our hearts and love because of what he accomplished for us, for you, for me – every one of us.

❦

That Jewish Passover meal helped me to understand much more clearly about the Last Supper. But there was something else also. One of the Jewish ladies there, a rather striking person, very humble and very quiet, had been in Belsen, that terrible concentration camp. I looked at her with great respect and I wondered how often at nights she must have suffered like Our Lord in his agony; suffered from fear, horror and terrible loneliness which in him mingled blood with sweat on his brow. She knew all that too, and over a number of years. And now, how much she must appreciate freedom and life, and relish the love of family and friends.

❦

A great celebration

On Maundy Thursday we celebrate that first occasion when Our Lord took bread and changed it into his body, took wine and changed it into his blood. That truth requires from us humility, which can only be his gift. I mean that humility of mind whereby we acknowledge in truth that what was once bread is now his body, what was once wine is now his blood. That is why we genuflect to pay honour to him in the Blessed Sacrament. Afterwards, when we pray at the altar of repose, we know that we are close to him in his suffering in the garden of Gethsemane, as close to him as Mary Magdalen was when she met him in the garden on that first Easter Sunday: this is the astonishing fact.

So, Maundy Thursday is when we renew our act of faith in that great truth, and recognise that in the Mass, which Jesus instigated at the Last Supper, we have the means given by him, to become involved in his passion, death and resurrection. For every Mass is a celebration of Good Friday and Easter Sunday, and Maundy Thursday was the day on which these two realities – his death and resurrection – were made available to us through the Mass. That great act which is both sacrifice and banquet is central to the life of the Church.

※

The courtesy of Christ

We recall also how Our Lord, at the Last Supper, got up and washed the feet of his apostles and in doing so showed us something about divine courtesy. Jesus reveals what is divine. He washed the feet of his disciples to show the kind of courtesy and regard which God has for us. That in itself is an astonishing thought and one that should occupy our thoughts and our prayers. If such divine courtesy can be shown to us, what can we show in return? Should we not match his courtesy, born of love for us, with courtesy and love in return? He showed us, too, that love, Christian charity, is not just a word to trip all too easily off our tongue, but one to move us to action and to service, especially of those who are poor and those in need.

❦

The altar of repose

Finally on Maundy Thursday there is the procession to the altar of repose, in which the Blessed Sacrament is carried to a quiet place where we can go, one by one, alone, to pray. There is a clear link between the two parts of the ceremony, for we shall never worship effectively unless we have learned to pray privately. We shall never serve our neighbour out of true love unless we have a personal relationship with Our Lord himself.

That quiet private prayer is not always easy, as Peter, James and John discovered. Like them, we fail too often to respond as we should to his question: 'Could you not watch one hour with me?' As we recall his agony in the garden and – dare we say it – recall his need of our presence with him, we should stay with him for a few moments, alone in prayer, our deep needs meeting his, and his wishes becoming ours. So when it is all over and there is nothing left but silence – a silence broken on Good Friday by that terrible cry 'Crucify him' – we should think about the presence of Jesus in our lives and what that means.

Good Friday

❧

Commemoration of the Lord's Passion

'My God, my God, why hast thou forsaken me?'

We hear those words proclaimed in the Gospel every year. Jesus was praying from Psalm 21. He found in that psalm the words that expressed his agony as he was slowly dying on the cross. He felt abandoned by his closest followers and by all who only a week before were singing a triumphant hosanna. Now they were shouting: 'Crucify him, crucify him.'

It is hard to be betrayed by a colleague and friend, such as Judas; sad to be unsupported by one very close to you, such as Peter. Even worse, the sense of being abandoned by God is the most terrifying of all. It means a terrible desolation of heart.

But Mary, his Mother, stood by the cross, with other women and John, the only apostle who had not fled. Jesus spoke to her: 'Woman, behold thy son' and to John: 'Son, behold thy Mother.' (John 19:26–7). She was there at the moment of his greatest crisis, unable to do other than be with him, sharing his agony, watching and waiting. Something of her was dying as he died, as happens when we lose one we love very much – a husband, a wife, a child, a friend. She is always there for us even if we are abandoned by all ⁄ and even apparently, though not in reality, by God.

❦

Consolation from Christ's suffering

How often do we hear of people crying out in pain, and especially in bewilderment, when they cannot understand why they must suffer. Suffering is so often a mystery. For much that is evil we can find quick answers: 'It is to do with sin', 'We are free to choose, thus there is always the possibility of sin. We can choose, and often do, to do wrong.' Such answers may help in some cases but not in all. Frequently we are left with the question 'Why?'

Then in the darkness a light begins to shine, just a small light, more of a flicker than full sunlight, but enough for me to say, 'I know where to look when still unable to see clearly.' If I look long enough at the figure of Christ dying on the cross I begin to see that his passion and death had a purpose which is directly related to our own suffering. For the suffering that Jesus endured provides consolation and guidance in our greatest pain. As we look at the cross we should venerate it and embrace it in our prayer. It will slowly give up its secret, not suddenly but over the years and Christ's suffering will lead us to new life.

Christ died, but he rose again from the dead, and that is our hope – hope which gives peace and joy, hope which gives courage to carry the cross daily in life. Forgiveness, the promise of future happiness with God, the realisation of his love – these are all part of hope, and the giving of hope is Easter's special gift.

The cross is the sign of victory and hope. On Good Friday we remember what it cost Our Lord to achieve that victory for us.

The Seven Last Words

❧

I once sat all night by the bedside of a dying monk. The effort he made to breathe was hard, the pain was great. In the early hours of the morning, as death seemed imminent, I noticed that he was struggling to speak. I approached as close as I could to catch his words, his last words. What was it he was trying to say? A message for his friends or his family? An anxiety in his mind compounding the pain in his body? Slowly, and with difficulty, I heard the words; they were not always clear, it is true. But I had as yet to dwell on their meaning and understand the full impact of what he had said. I jotted them down on a piece of paper, and afterwards – after his death and burial – I began to think about these words and heard through them his voice, a message of love and hope.

I thought of Jesus: in agony from fear and apprehension in the garden the night before he died; in pain from the flogging he had received and the crown of thorns piercing the skin of his head; in anguish because he was betrayed by Judas and abandoned by his close friends. And now, on Good Friday, after the long and painful journey up the hill called Calvary, he was crucified. Dying a most cruel and agonising death, he had still words to speak – his last words.

Those who stood by the cross – his Mother, a few other women, concerned to be with him and brave indeed, and John, the only one not to flee – listened and heard the words come, haltingly no doubt and with great effort. These were precious words for his Mother and his friends and they remembered them, spoke about them, recorded them. These words from the lips of this dying man were a message from him who was both God and man.

Long after his death and burial, his friends down the ages have dwelt on the meaning of his last words and heard through them his voice, bearing a message of love and hope.

❦

'Father, forgive them, for they know not what they do.'

They drove nails through his hands and his feet, to secure him on the cross. He had suffered the scourging, and thorns battered into his head. Insults, humiliations, taunting – and now the pain in hands and feet as the nails tore through his flesh. The pain in his body accompanied now the agony of his mind, the agony that was his in the garden on the night before.

And yet he forgives. He forgives them for what they are doing, for the pain they are inflicting. He is desperate, almost, to find an excuse: 'they know not what they are doing.' Were they just obeying orders, doing what they were told by other men who were anxious to kill this prophet? Can these soldiers be excused for their part in so grievous a crime?

Jesus forgives, ignoring, so it would seem, the question that we ask. 'Father, forgive them; for they know not what they do.' Thus he prays, those words of his spoken not from weakness, but from the strength of love which he has for us.

There is a deeper truth here for us to learn. It is that God seeks always to forgive. He will look for every reason to forgive, to make excuses for us, to understand. Nonetheless he looks into our hearts to find sorrow, or at least the beginning of it. He expects us to be sorry and to say so; to recognise the wrong we have done. There is comfort in remembering that he will not spurn a humble and contrite heart.

❦

'This day thou shalt be with me in paradise.'

He was suffering, too, the good thief. Abandoned, with no family to comfort or friends to help. Who remembers a common thief, dying on a cross for the wrong he has done? Who will stand by him, claim his friendship? That thief prayed: 'Remember me when thou comest into thy kingdom.' Sad, sorry, repentant, anxious, broken almost – he sought to make amends. The answer comes: 'This day thou shalt be with me in paradise.'

This day, could he have expected that? When his final agony came, he was at peace. Death came, not a foe, but a gentle friend.

A humble, contrite heart is never spurned. Sorrow for sin is never too late, wrongdoing never so great that forgiveness will be refused. Others may ignore, forget, lose interest. God never does. He cannot forget or cease to wait for that word of sorrow for our wrongdoing, a word that heralds our entry into his kingdom. Do not despair or give up hope. However far you may have wandered, whatever wrong you may have done, despair must never be a word you know. He wants us, more than we have ever wanted him, or ever could.

'This day you will be with me in paradise.' This will be said to you when you pray: 'Remember me . . . '

❦

'Woman, behold thy son. Son, behold thy Mother.'

When his side was pierced, blood and water flowed. Water, with its cleansing and life-giving power, makes us one with Christ, the sons and daughters of his Father. Blood was shed for us, to redeem us from sin and given to us to nourish and strengthen.

The Church was born from his side, as Eve from Adam's. In the waters of the font it is reborn and from the chalice sustained.

❦

Mary his Mother stood with John, and with Mary and Salome too. A mother mourning her Son, suffering and sharing his pain, she listened to his word and pondered it in her heart, as was her wont. 'Woman, behold thy son.'

His hour had come and so had hers, her soul pierced by the sword of suffering, as Simeon had foretold. As if in labour, she was now mother again, Mother of the Church – Mother of those reborn in the font of Baptism and nourished by his body and blood, the water and blood that came from the wound in his side.

'Son, behold thy Mother.' He took her to his own, John, the beloved disciple, to provide for her needs, as she would provide for his. There would be a space for her in his home perhaps; most surely a space for her in his heart.

※

Jesus cried out with a loud voice: 'My God, my God, why hast thou forsaken me?'

When in the mind there is only darkness and fear, when there is only emptiness and none to help or console; when life has only death to offer to escape from pain and to be at rest – then we cry out in anguish to God to come and help, to console.

When silence reigns and no answer comes, we are lost, abandoned, and know only fear. 'My God, my God, why hast thou forsaken me?' That prayer from the psalm conveys the depth of sadness, the anguish of the soul of Christ – forsaken, forgotten even, by God himself.

It was his prayer as he trod the pilgrim way through despair and the dark vale of tears and anguish to that hope – God's gift to those who feel forsaken. It is then that they must abandon their hearts to him when they see no point in doing so.

A gift when all is darkness, emptiness too, is precious in the eyes of a Father who seeks above all our trusting in him when that trust is hard to give. But give it, and the emptiness is filled, inner wounds healed and peace achieved.

⁂

'I thirst.'

He had endured so much, and now the agonising pain of hanging, held only by hands and feet, his body stretched and racked. He was thirsty, his lips dry, his palate parched: he longed to drink.

There was another thirst, and from a different pain. He had been betrayed by his friend, by Judas. He had been rejected by his own, those who had supported him.

Judas, oh Judas – betrayal hurts more when the one who betrays has received much from the one he seeks to betray. Betrayal hurts, and hurts very much.

A few days ago they hailed him with palms and song. Now they curse him, reproach him, seemingly hate him. He loved them and he still does. He still loves Judas, Judas who has betrayed him.

His human heart pined for all of us, and still does. That heart of his revealed a divine thirst, God's thirst for you and me. Christ, who is not only man but God as well, speaks in human words of realities of God known to us only through the words and actions we can understand.

We who can so easily betray, or at least lose our way by forgetting or ignoring him who thirsts for us, for you and for me – what shall we give, you and I, to him who thirsts for us?

> A sweet cooling drink,
> we call it love,
> to quench the thirst of him
> who first loved us.

❦

'It is finished.'

Obedient to his Father's will, he has accomplished the work that he was given: to take our pain, and death as well, upon himself. Death, the wages of sin, was borne by him, ever pure and sinless.

He had become man in order to endure the pain known by many in wars, famine, earthquakes too. In the soul as well: mental anguish, adversity, loss of reason. You know suffering? So did he. Have you felt abandoned, even by God? So did he. Have you been humiliated, despised, insulted? So was he. Perhaps you have been misunderstood, vilified. So was he. He, too, walked in the dark, entered the tomb lifeless and defeated, vanquished.

But death could not win. His body would not be imprisoned. He rose again, victorious over death and sin. He has made all things new. It is finished, the work is done.

There will still be wars, famines, earthquakes, and other kinds of suffering too, which come in the wake of sin. Mental anguish, anxiety, loss of reason are still part of human living, but now different. He has hidden in human pain the seed of divine life. Hope is now hidden in human despair, joy concealed in human sadness. Anguish, anxiety, the ravages of war and famine, all hide within themselves a rich reward, a precious treasure – life hidden with Christ in God for the sharers in his passion.

It is not for me to read the mind of God, nor to pronounce on his ways. Much is hidden, little revealed. Yet, though it is hard at times to see, love is his reason. This, and only this, inspires his deeds.

'Into your hands, Lord, I commend my spirit.'

The end was near. He was in great distress, overcome by pain, his mind in turmoil. He had no choice but to abandon himself into the outstretched hands of his heavenly Father.

His prayer 'Into your hands I commend my spirit' was his leap of love from life on earth to life with the

Father. That was the password into God's presence, into those hands, those safe hands stretching out to receive his weary soul. Not for him the fear of judgement, for in him there was no sin.

For us there may be fear indeed, and rightly so if arrogance, pride, avarice or cruelty have reigned in our lives and are not forgiven because we have not sorrowed. We can refuse to be lifted by those hands, remaining self-sufficient, steeped in evil and empty. Our judgement will be swift for we stand self-condemned.

Those of us who have not turned away, but in spite of failure, weakness and sin have not rejected him, will approach trembling, nervous no doubt, but reassured and at peace as we tell the story of our lives which only he can understand. He knows the burdens we have carried, the struggles too, the reasons for our failure and our sins. He will whisper into our ear, 'Come'. Then we shall enter, happy, and ready to wait until purified and made worthy to be with him and to rest forever in those loving hands.

Holy Saturday: The Easter Vigil

🌿

On Holy Saturday there is stillness, silence, a sense of emptiness almost. It is a time of waiting, of expectation, of preparation for the great celebration that night, and as the day progresses and the sun goes down, we start our celebration in darkness. Sometimes I think that the darkness that descends on our churches matches in some manner the darkness in the minds of many of us.

Just as at the moment when light shines again we have a new view of familiar surroundings, perhaps after darkness we tend to see things differently, in a new light. When light is present there is recognition of what is there.

It is a festival of light on Holy Saturday and there is one light above all for which we must pray, and that is the light of the Holy Spirit. In the Word of God, as we listen to it then, familiar passages will be seen in a new light; familiar ceremonial highlighted by the celebration of Mass, well known to us but seen in a new light. So on Holy Saturday, a day of waiting and expectation, we should pray that our minds be given that light to recognise in him who died and rose again from the dead our true Saviour, Jesus Christ Our Lord.

⚜

The light of Christ in a world of darkness

Darkness is unfriendly. Darkness is cold; it means loneliness. It makes us uncertain, fretful, uneasy, suspicious. Darkness is hostile even, and worse, much worse, darkness is a world without God.

Light is different and especially so when it comes from a fire. Fire can be hostile too, and devastatingly so. But more often fire is friendly, it gives warmth. It draws others to it and takes central place in company. Light is friendly too, it guides, shows us the way, lights up the path, comforts.

Darkness is always to be shunned, but light and fire should be celebrated, and this is what happens in the Easter vigil. The Easter fire lit at the entrance to a cathedral or a church is like a great explosion of warmth and light overcoming the darkness. It reminds me always of that burning bush which manifested to Moses the presence of God.

Where there is light, where there is warmth, there God is. The light and warmth of the fire are transferred, as it were, to the paschal candle. The priest or deacon sings 'Lumen Christi', the light of Christ, and we answer 'Thanks be to God', thereby acknowledging that Christ is the true light of the world. Darkness is a

[109]

world without God. He came to dispel the darkness. Darkness and coldness are powerful symbols of the society in which we live – symbols of a world which neglects God because without God the world is dark and cold. It is a terrible thing when there is darkness in our minds and coldness in our hearts. Light in our minds is the sense of God, the truth about him and the truth that comes from him. We call it faith. Warmth in the heart is a wanting of God, a desiring of him. It is the beginning of love. We call it charity.

❦

Baptism: carrying the light of Christ

Baptism is a vital theme of our liturgy at Easter, a time when we renew our baptismal promises. At baptism we received the precious gift of faith and received the warmth of charity in our hearts – the Holy Spirit present and active in our minds and hearts. As we renew our promises we hold small white candles to remind us of Christ's gift of light and love, and to remind us too that we are to carry the light of Christ into the world where we live and work.

We have a responsibility in virtue of our baptism and confirmation to be a light of Christ, dispelling where we can, and how best we can, the darkness and coldness of a world without God.

Easter Sunday

✤

There is an account in the New Testament of St
Peter's instruction on the Christian faith to a
man called Cornelius and his household (Acts
10). Who was Cornelius? He was a Roman soldier
stationed in Caesarea. He was in charge of about a hundred men in the army of occupation. We are told he was
a devout and God-fearing man who gave generously to
Jewish causes, so he was obviously a friend of the local
Jewish community. We are also told that he prayed constantly to God. He was not a Christian at that point, but
was clearly looking for something, a man whose religious
instinct had been awakened, no longer just dormant. But
he had never heard of Jesus, or at least only indirectly.

However, he received a special message from God
and was told to seek out Peter. Peter was not all that
keen on seeing Cornelius simply because he was not a
Jew, But then he too received a special message and was
told to receive Cornelius. So they met. Peter instructed
Cornelius in the Christian faith and eventually the
Roman and his family all became Christians, followers
of Christ. Peter had to explain that Jesus had been

killed 'by hanging him on a tree', yet – and here was the important and difficult part – 'three days afterwards, God raised him to life'.

I wonder what went through Cornelius' head at that moment. Was he unconvinced? Sceptical? Why, people don't die and then come back to life, certainly not in an advanced and sophisticated society such as that of the Roman Empire at the time. But Peter went on: yes, God *did* raise Jesus to life, and what is more – Peter hammered the point home – God allowed him to be seen, not by everybody but by certain witnesses chosen beforehand. It strikes me that Peter was being a little modest in his claim about the number of people who saw Jesus risen and alive. St Paul, writing to the Corinthians said that on one occasion the risen Christ was seen by 500 people at the same time, and added: 'If you doubt it, you can verify the fact because most of those who saw Christ on that occasion are still alive.' St Paul was writing very early on and knew what he was saying.

But, to return to Cornelius, Peter is at pains to point out, 'now we are those witnesses – we have eaten and drunk with him after his resurrection from the dead'. He could have gone further – perhaps he did – and told Cornelius how he had seen the empty tomb, how he had run there with St John. John himself could not refrain from saying that he got there first! They both ran and saw the empty tomb. Moreover, they saw the linen cloth which had been wrapped round the dead body of Jesus, and they saw that the cloth which had covered his face was in a different place.

They had not expected to find the tomb empty. They had failed to understand the teaching of Scripture that 'Christ must rise from the dead'. St John is at pains to point that out. He and Peter had gone to the burial site only because Mary of Magdala had rushed to tell them what she had seen – an empty tomb.

Where was the body? Who had stolen it? I can see those questions playing in Cornelius' mind. What had happened? Obviously someone had taken it, someone had stolen it. That was the rumour. This had unnerved the people responsible for killing Jesus. So they bribed the soldiers who were guarding the tomb to say they had fallen asleep, and while they were asleep someone came and rolled the stone away and took the body. They took the money and spread the story – a very far-fetched story. But the tomb was empty and something very important had happened, because the disciples remembered what Jesus had said: 'Yes, on the third day I will rise again.'

Where, Cornelius insisted, was the body? Where was Jesus? He was told by St Peter that many had seen him alive, but his appearance was often very strange. Mary of Magdala thought he was the gardener. The two disciples walking on the way to Emmaus failed to recognise him. They saw him, but all seemed different now. Jesus had changed, acting after the resurrection quite differently from the way he had acted before he died. But he was still the real Jesus, risen from the dead.

❧

Witnesses to the risen Christ

Now the apostles' lives were beginning to change also. Once the Holy Spirit had come down upon them they were transformed and went on saying again and again, 'Jesus has risen from the dead'. The truth of Jesus Christ, true God and true man, is what they preached and it is to that that they gave witness. Cornelius was received into the Christian community and he too, and his household, became witnesses to the fact that the tomb was empty and Jesus Christ was alive, risen from the dead.

Indeed, many people joined together in community simply because Jesus Christ, true God and true man, had risen from the dead. A community grew up out of an acknowledgment of that fact. Even more than that, there were people prepared to be witnesses, even to the extent of losing their lives – becoming martyrs for Jesus. I think of Cornelius going back to his family and reminding them of what they have learned – that they must be witnesses by the way they live, and that Jesus, who had risen from the dead, was to be their leader. They were to learn about the Gospel, follow the things Jesus said and do as he bid.

Everything was different – and so it has to be for us. As we come together at Easter in the great act of worship, we listen to the Word of God proclaimed. Then we must go back to our households and tell them that we, too, should be witnesses to Christ, to the Gospel, to the Church. We must be witnesses because out there

there are thousands and thousands of people who do not know Christ, yet are searching, wanting. The religious instinct in every person, perhaps, in our time, is beginning to awaken. Who can tell them where to find the truth but those who belong to the Christian community which believes in Christ who died and rose from the dead? That is the task for all of us, to be witnesses to that fact and to all that follows from it.

The Easter Message

※

On Easter morning especially, two images come to my mind. They sum up the story of Easter. The first is of Christ abandoned and dying on the cross. The other is of the empty tomb, a sign that death has been overcome. Christ died that we might live. He laid down his life to show his love.

Easter challenges us each year. Do we believe that Christ truly rose from the dead? Belief in the resurrection is the bedrock of Christianity. It is at the heart of the Easter message.

※

Life with God

In the risen Christ death has lost its hold over mankind. Death is not for us the end of the story. It is the beginning of a new chapter. There is life after death. It is life with God. The purpose of our present life is to prepare for that.

Easter is not only concerned with life after death. It

has much to say about life here on earth. Life matters. Human life is both of the body and of the spirit; in our present state each depends on the other. Life depends on love. Life gives love its real meaning and its purpose. Our Easter faith assures us that life will overcome death and love will triumph over hatred.

Easter does not take suffering away from us, nor does it save us from physical death. But suffering and death are now different, because Christ suffered and died. Indeed, before Christ rose from the dead there was only despair at the centre of pain. Now, and because of Christ, there is hope. When we know pain or depression, when we feel abandoned, or when we are dying, we remember that Christ had the same experiences. Our suffering brings us closer to Christ and closer to God.

Epilogue:
The Liturgy of the Eucharist

🦋

Our Saviour, at the Last Supper on the night on which he was betrayed, instituted the eucharistic Sacrifice of his Body and Blood whereby he might perpetuate the sacrifice of the cross throughout the ages until he should come, and moreover, entrust to the Church, his beloved Bride, a memorial of his death and resurrection: the sacrament of love, the sign of unity, the bond of charity, the paschal banquet, in which Christ is received, our mind and soul are filled with grace and a pledge is given us of glory to come.
(Sacred Constitution on the Sacred Liturgy, no. 47)

I watched him as he came to that most solemn moment of the Mass. He bent over the altar, just a little, and holding up the Host, he spoke, quite slowly but so clearly. He said: 'This is my Body which will be given up for you.' Then he raised the Host above his head for all to see, went down on one knee to venerate what with those words had been transformed. We all bowed, one with him in his silent worship. And so with the chalice filled with wine, but the words were different, of course. 'This is my Blood, the new and everlasting covenant, shed for you and for the forgiveness of sins.' Again we bowed. Then he spoke again, indeed almost cried out, a note of triumph in his voice, 'the mystery of faith'. What we had heard and seen were words beautifully said and actions elegantly performed. Something else within us carried us beyond what we had heard and seen the priest do. He had changed that bread into the Body of Christ, that wine into his Blood. We saw only bread and wine. Our senses could take us no further. Another gift, like a sixth sense, came to our rescue – faith.

Though we saw only bread and wine, we knew they were no longer such, but now his Body and his Blood, Christ's Body, Christ's Blood. We had discovered this mystery of our faith: the reality, which lies beyond our understanding, signified and accomplished by the words the priest had said. Before calling us to proclaim our faith in the true presence of Christ's Body and Blood, the priest had said, 'Do this in memory of me'. Remembering – that was a key concept for the Jewish people; it is equally so for Christians. But first, note how the priest had said, *my Body* and *my Blood*. He spoke thus because Christ was speaking and acting through the priest; Christ the High Priest was using this frail human instrument to achieve his noble purpose.

Our faith continued to take us where our unaided reason could not go. Where and how far? The years rolled back. There he was with his twelve closest followers. They were celebrating the Passover. This was the night when every Jew must live again the experience of being freed from slavery and oppression. 'Why this thanksgiving?' a child would ask. It is our duty, the child was told, to recall our departure from Egypt, our crossing of the Red Sea, our wandering in the desert. They remembered, not only to be part of the memory, but to make that memory real for the present. They celebrated the Passover meal to make present in some manner the saving act by God of his chosen people. At some point Jesus took bread and wine and thus gave to that Passover meal a new significance and a different meaning. 'Do this in memory of me', he said.

What are we to recall? We watched the priest at the altar, the bread now changed into Christ's Body, the wine into his Blood. Then we remembered how Jesus had been sad, how the betrayal by Judas set off that train of events which ended with his death on Calvary. That was the hour for which he had come, a great mystery. The Mass makes that 'hour', the death and resurrection of Christ, present in every age. God who became man died on a cross that we might be freed from sin and its consequences, death. We can but stand silently, as it were, at the foot of the cross with Mary, his mother, with John, the beloved disciple, and some women followers. 'Silently', I said, because the enormity of what took place on Calvary is too much for our limited understanding. Faith can take us so far, but not all the way. But should we not, every one of us, have been there as he was dying, catching from the words he spoke some consolation for ourselves?

'Father forgive them ...'

'This day you will be with me in paradise ...'

'Woman, behold your son ...'

We could not be there, hence the gift of another Passover celebration to go on for all time, the Mass. It is Calvary brought to us, his Body and Blood lying separated on the altar. He still says – and asks us to join him – 'into your hands, Lord, I commend my spirit'. His sacrifice on Calvary is made present for us through signs given by him at that Last Supper. Every time we celebrate Mass, it is in memory of him. Our offering of ourselves, our sacrifice is joined to his, and from his receives its value.

Then, remarkably, he gives us his Body to eat and his Blood to drink. 'I am the living bread which comes down from heaven; if any one eats of this bread, he will live forever; and the bread that I shall give for the life of the world is my flesh ... unless you eat the flesh of the Son of Man and drink his blood, you have no life in you.' (John 6:51, 53)

It would not be so unless he had risen from the dead. The mystery of faith includes the resurrection. Unless Christ is risen, our faith is in vain. One day Peter had been enabled to walk on the water, until his trust in Jesus began to weaken. Then he began to sink. It is the same with us when doubts are received into our sceptical minds and we begin to sink. No, he could not have risen from the dead. People do not do that. No, he could not ask us to eat his Body and drink his Blood.

Then a word of rebuke, tinged with some sadness, 'Would you, too, go away?' It is for us to answer: 'Lord, to whom shall we go? You have the words of eternal life; and we have believed, and have come to know, that you are the Holy One of God.' (John 6:67–9)

I shall be there again next Sunday (maybe more often) for it is only by attending week after week that I can begin to explore the mystery, and become part of it.

One day I wondered if there were a liturgy in heaven. The question seemed an idle one, for how can we know? Then I recalled how the Book of Revelation described the worshipping of God by all the angels and saints.

And between the throne and the four living creatures and among the elders, I saw a Lamb standing, as though it had been slain, with seven horns and with seven eyes, which are the seven spirits of God sent out into all the earth; and he went and took the scroll from the right hand of him who was seated on the throne. And when he had taken the scroll, the four living creatures and the twenty-four elders fell down before the Lamb, each holding a harp, and with golden bowls full of incense, which are the prayers of the saints; and they sang a new song, saying, 'Worthy art thou to take the scroll and to open its seals, for thou wast slain and by thy blood didst ransom men for God from every tribe and tongue and people and nation, and hast made them a kingdom and priests to our God, and they shall reign on

[123]

earth.' Then I looked, and I heard around the throne and the living creatures and the elders the voice of many angels, numbering myriads of myriads and thousands of thousands, saying with a loud voice, 'Worthy is the Lamb who was slain, to receive power and wealth and wisdom and might and honour and glory and blessing!' And I heard every creature in heaven and on earth and under the earth and in the sea, and all therein, saying, 'To him who sits upon the throne and to the Lamb be blessing and honour and glory and might for ever and ever!' And the four living creatures said, 'Amen!' and the elders fell down and worshipped.

(Revelation 5:6–14)

There is food for thought and prayer. We join in that great act of worship every time we celebrate Mass: the 'Lamb standing, as though it had been slain' lies on the altar, the consecrated bread and consecrated wine.

Watch the priest at his task and especially when he changes, through power given to him by Christ, the bread and wine. With the eyes of faith see Christ celebrating the Passover, dying on the cross, coming forth from the tomb, and entering into the Holy of Holies to celebrate the eternal liturgy of Heaven. His death, resurrection and ascension are each recalled every time we 'do this in memory of him'.